CROSS STITCH
CALLIGRAPHY

A Practical Guide
to Creating Samplers, Monograms
& Personalized Gifts

Iva Polansky

LONDON   NEW YORK   SYDNEY   TORONTO

This book is dedicated to my beloved aunt, Fran,
who sternly supervised my very first stitches

Photographs by Christopher Cormack unless
otherwise stated

This edition published 1994 by BCA by arrangement with
Kyle Cathie Limited

CN 6051

Edited by Caroline Taggart
Designed by Clare Clements
Charts by Nigel Partridge
Alphabets by Anthony Duke
Photograph on page 6 by Jacqui Hurst

Printed and bound in Great Britain by
Bath Press Colourbooks.

CONTENTS

ION POLANSKY

NEEDLE *Calligraphy*

Create personalized gifts,
monograms, samplers, signs,
quotations, greeting cards,
wedding or birth records...

INTRODUCTION

'A picture is worth a thousand words,' said Comenius, the great 16th-century teacher. True. Almost true, that is. Pictures are rich in details that stimulate our imagination. We perceive shapes, colours, textures, moods and, possibly, a message. But here the power of pictures fades. The domain of the concrete belongs to words. Only words can convey the exact information as to who, where, when and why.

Look around you at jumble sales. Chances are that you will find stacks of anonymous embroideries, some of them very beautiful, but hardly a signed or dated sampler, a family tree or a wedding record. Why?

The answer is simple. These items 'belong'. They are a part of a family's history and, as such, deserve the status of heirlooms. They are not casually thrown away when someone moves house. However crude their execution, old samplers fetch high prices at antique auctions. Again, names and words have a magical effect on us. Our imagination is awakened when we read the often misspelt pious messages of all the Catherines, Elizabeths and Janes of centuries past. Who were they? Were they as industrious and God-fearing as their samplers would have us believe? What was their life like? What were their dreams and ambitions? We will never know. But we are intrigued, curious. Such is the power of words.

This book is an answer to my frustrated attempts at calligraphy. I love letters. I am thrilled by their shapes and by their ability to capture ideas. Calligraphy is an art that has always attracted me. Unfortunately, creating beautiful letter forms requires an adventurous hand guided by a steady rhythm, two opposing qualities that must be in perfect harmony. Mistakes are not forgiven in calligraphy. Hours of intense work often come to nought, for a single lapse in concentration can spoil the whole effort just as the project nears its end.

That doesn't happen in counted-thread embroidery. There is time to plan, to change the proportions, to add and eliminate at will. We know precisely how the result will look before sewing the first stitch. Although the smoothly flowing strokes of handwriting cannot be reproduced in counted-thread embroidery, needle calligraphy has its own rewards. It is impossible to achieve the combination of the print-like quality of the letters and the special texture of needlework by any other means.

I hope this book will encourage you to spend hours of pure delight creating personalized designs for yourself, your family, your friends. Words and letters can make any object special. We all respond favourably to a monogrammed gift, for it speaks of loving care. It makes us feel important – and what a sweet feeling that is! A wedding record, for instance, does not require a great financial outlay, yet it will successfully compete with the most splendid gifts others may offer. A personalized greeting card speaks clearly of your affection and may end up framed while the mass-produced ones are tossed into the wastepaper basket. With the new speedy technique that you will learn in this book, many small projects can be completed in a couple of days. Start today and enjoy yourself!

THE EVOLUTION OF WESTERN LETTERING

No one disputes the fact that the Latin alphabet – the alphabet we use today – is based on Greek characters. Even an untrained eye can detect familiar shapes while scanning a Greek inscription such as the one found in Abu Simbel some 26 centuries ago. Let's add the fact that the word *alphabet* is a composite of Alpha and Beta, the first two letters of the Greek alphabet, and that should dispel any lingering doubt.

THE ROMAN PERIOD

These Greek characters were first introduced to the Italian peninsula by the Etruscans, who lived between the rivers Arno and Tiber or, approximately, in today's Tuscany. Their civilization, the most refined west of Greece, was later entirely absorbed by the Romans. These uncultured but clever bullies were willing to learn whenever they could spare some time from the more pressing business of importuning their neighbours. As Latin was phonetically different from Greek, the Romans adopted only 21 of the 24 Greek letters and added two of their own to make a total of 23. The three missing letters of the modern alphabet, J, U and W, date only from the 16th or 17th century.

Given the perishable nature of the early Roman writing surfaces – more about these later – the first

LEFT *Detail from Trajan's Column, Rome, AD 114. Considered the highest form of* scriptura monumentalis, *these Trajan capitals have served, ever since, as a point of reference for lettering design (*Mansell Collection*).*

BELOW *Greek inscription at Abu Simbel, about 600 BC*

steps in the evolution of the Latin alphabet can be traced only by studying inscriptions carved in stone. Over 150,000 of these are dispersed around the vast territory once ruled by the Romans, so there is no shortage of historic back-up.

A rough, dynamic nation of conquerors, builders and administrators, the Romans were not artistically inclined. Compared to the aesthetic perfection of the Greeks of the same age, their artistic achievements are rather negligible. Consequently, it took hundreds of years for the Roman alphabet to evolve into the majestic, well-balanced, classic forms we now admire. Ironically, the Greeks were in part responsible for the improvement. At that time, about 200 BC, the Romans could finally sit back and contemplate what they had achieved so far by way of conquering the world. Pleased as they were, they decided to reward themselves with some refinement. As they had no illusions about their own artistic worth, they imported a large number of Greek statues for their rapidly improving dwellings, decorated – of course – after the Greek fashion. And, in case they needed more, they also imported Greek artists, many of them in the convenient form of slaves.

Thus the stage was set for the emergence of the sophisticated form of classic Roman alphabet. The *scriptura monumentalis* – 'monumental writing' – was used for inscriptions on public buildings and statues of gods or emperors. It reached perfection in the first century AD. Both the layout and the shape of the letters bear the touch of highly trained professionals. Usually, three specialists were responsible for the production of an inscription. The first was the author of the text. Then came the *ordinator*, a graphic artist who had to compose the design and draw it on the stone. The last of the trio, the *lapidarius* or stone worker, carved the design with all the precision he could muster. However, because the chisel was wider than some of the letters, for instance the I or the top and bottom portions of H, the *lapidarius* had no choice but to make the horizontal lines a bit larger. This, accidentally, gave birth to the serifs, those ingenious 'extra bits' on the letters still in use in many typefaces today. Although, at first, the Romans had no appreciation of serifs and disguised them by progressively enlarging the body of the letter so that it could meet the serif in a graceful curve, it soon became evident that serifs visually stabilized the letters and helped to give the text a calm and even appearance.

Given the limited space the *ordinator* often had to deal with and the rather intransigent nature of the *scriptura monumentalis* characters, all sorts of clever schemes had to be devised in order to fit the text into a specific area. Abbreviations and ligatures (letters joined together or overlapping each other) were used when a long text had to be squeezed into a short line. On the other hand, fillers and appropriate spacing

Roman inscription, Aquinum, AD 145–160. Fitting a text into a limited space has always presented a challenge. Observe how the designer resolved the problem of squeezing in the word CAPELLANUS. *The Romans were used to abbreviations (*LEG:AUG: *stands for* Legatus Augustus, *'august ambassador'.*

between letters and words expanded a text if it was too short. In the inscription bearing the name of Julius Geminus Capellanus, a Roman legate from Aquinum, all the aforementioned devices were used. With a lot of ingenuity, the artist created a solid bloc of text with perfectly aligned margins.

The *scriptura monumentalis*, as its name indicates, was used for works of some standing. For less formal use the Romans developed a leaner and faster alphabet. The *scriptura actuaria* or 'clerk's writing' was at first usually painted on walls. In the absence of newspapers, wall inscriptions were the only way of informing the public about forthcoming cultural events such as feeding Christians to wild beasts. Electoral signs and advertising found in the ruins of Pompeii constitute a proof that we are not the only civilization plagued by such things.

The advantage of the condensed forms of the *scriptura actuaria* was seized upon by the *ordinatores*, who always had problems with fitting fat letters into narrow spaces. A carved version of the painted alphabet soon found its way on to the stone. In some inscriptions the most important first lines were carved in the old fashion and the rest increasingly received the new treatment. Others were entirely composed of the condensed alphabet.

We have now reached the period of Roman history from which originated the first surviving handwritten documents. The later development of lettering was directly influenced by written forms and it is therefore important to mention these early styles. But, before doing so, let's have a look at the writing materials the Romans used.

The gifted Caius Plinius (AD 23–79), soldier, admiral, procurator, scientist and writer, informs us that the earliest writing surface was made of thin sheets of lead which were kept rolled when not in use. Since no specimens of these lead sheets survive, we can only speculate that the writing was engraved with a sharp instrument. We know that this is what happened later with wax tablets. These were actually made of wood, framed and covered with a thin coat of wax. Two, three or more were joined with leather straps to form a folding writing surface. The *stilus*, a sharp instrument for writing on wax, had a flattened end with which an existing text could be erased and the wax reused. While handy for letters, short notes and other informal use, wax tablets could not serve for official documents.

The Roman clerk who had to record an official text needed a piece of papyrus. Made by gluing and pressing narrow strips of a reed grown in Egypt, papyrus was rough and brittle. Hardly an ideal writing surface, yet the whole Roman administration was entirely dependent on this imported commodity. No wonder the Romans were so keen on conquering Egypt!

However, before Caesar met Cleopatra and Cleopatra met Mark Antony, a major development had taken place in Pergamon, a Greek city in Asia Minor. For some obscure reason, an Egyptian king prohibited the export of papyrus to Pergamon. At first, the Pergamonians were desperate. Theirs was a very cultured city, with a library that rivalled the one in Alexandria (that is to say, one of the largest in the world), and they needed a lot of papyrus. Necessity being the mother of invention, they devised a new writing surface which became known as *pergamenum* to the Romans and parchment to us.

Parchment was a great improvement on papyrus. The inner side of split sheepskin of which it was made was subjected to a long process of refinement that resulted in a smooth and durable material. Writing became an enjoyable experience as the pen glided over the even surface. The only drawback of parchment was its high price. At least the Romans could import it duty free because, needless to say, they had conquered a large chunk of Asia Minor, including Pergamon.

While we are at it, let's mention paper even though it did not appear in the West until long after the period we are discussing. Paper is a Chinese invention brought to Europe in the tenth century by the Arabs who had invaded most of the Iberian peninsula, that is today's Spain and Portugal. Cheaper and faster to produce than parchment and the finer vellum, another animal-skin product, paper became the most widely used writing support. In the 15th century, following the invention of printing, the demand for paper grew steadily. In 1798, the Frenchman Nicolas-Louis Robert invented a paper-making machine, but mass production of paper had to wait some 50 more years.

Back to Rome. The heart of a Roman publishing house was the *scriptorium*, where dozens of slaves repeatedly copied the same text. If this does not sound like much fun, consider the fact that each scribe was issued a small portion of the text to be copied again and again. This could go on for years as long as the manuscript was in demand. Perhaps the familiar expression 'I'm slaving over a manuscript', so dear to all authors, goes back to these cruel times.

Because of the slow copying process and the high cost of the material, books were a luxury very few could afford. However, people had access to public libraries where books could be rented and taken home for reading. Storage and handling were somewhat awkward because Roman books were actually scrolls of papyrus or parchment. Despite the fact that the first bound books appeared towards the end of the first century, scrolls continued to be produced for another 500 years, although less and less frequently.

Broadly speaking, the early Roman scripts can be divided into two main categories, formal and informal. Representing the first is the *capitalis rustica* or 'rustic capitals', a condensed alphabet similar to the *scriptura actuaria*. The adjective 'rustic' is not employed here in the sense of 'awkward' or 'artless'. Rather, it expresses a freedom of movement, lightness and fluidity, as opposed to the strict and majestic forms of the *scriptura monumentalis*.

Used for documents and manuscripts, rustic capitals were nevertheless very orderly compared to the rapid, chaotic strokes of the *scriptura cursiva* or 'flowing writing'. Very few examples of the Roman cursive script survive. Most of those that do come from the

Rustic capitals

ABOVE *Roman cursive script, Pompeii, before AD 79*

abcdEFGhiLmɲo pqɲrTu

ABOVE *Roman bookhand, third to fourth century*

UNCIALS

ABOVE *A later form of uncials, sixth to ninth century*

ruins of Pompeii, where they were found as scribblings on walls and wax tablets. Apparently, there are specialists called paleographs who are able to make sense out of the mess opposite, but I suspect they have a standing prescription for a headache remedy.

Although lacking in legibility and aesthetic value, the cursive style had a significant influence on the further development of writing. Up to this point, the official Roman script was composed of letters written within a fixed height above the base line. This began to change between the second and third centuries, when the ascending and descending strokes of the cursive infiltrated official documents and books. The resulting *scriptura mixta* or 'mixed writing' was an interesting half-breed of capitals and cursive. The letters began to expand in width, assuming square proportions.

The Roman bookhand developed even further during the fourth century and turned into a graceful, curvaceous and very popular script called *scriptura uncialis*. The *uncia* or ounce was a twelfth part of a standard measure, and it is believed that the name originated because a standard line of text could accommodate only about twelve of these large letters. Over 700 surviving specimens from all over Western Europe testify to the popularity of this style. The finest examples come from England (the *Lindisfarne Gospels*, seventh century) and Ireland (*The Book of Kells*, eighth century).

Uncials are traditionally associated with early Christianity and the spread of the new faith throughout Europe. We are now leaving behind the disintegrated Roman Empire and are moving northwards to the heart of Europe, from which came the next impulse in the development of letter forms.

ESTABLISHING AN OFFICIAL SCRIPT

By this time Europe had sunk deeply into the Dark Ages. Gone was the refined way of living, the relative security, the law and order maintained by the Romans. However, Latin remained the official language of church and diplomacy and therefore that of written documents. In an age when even the kings could not read and write, only the clergy carried the light of learning. Which is to say that science and secular art

were put on a back burner, where they remained for a long time. The cultural centres, that is monasteries and other religious institutions, were thinly disseminated. This isolation caused a parallel development of regional writing styles. Uncorrected by a central power, these became so corrupt as to be practically illegible to those who were not familiar with their shapes. The situation was intolerable and something had to be done about it.

What emerged to solidify this chaotic, post-Roman continent was the Carolingian Empire, with its seat in Aachen, northern Germany. Charlemagne, king of the Franks and founder of this new Christian empire, never mastered the art of writing – although it is said that he tried hard from the age of forty. But he understood its importance as a means of communication, especially as the territory he ruled grew in size. The most learned man Charlemagne had at hand was Alcuin of York, Bishop of Tours and master of the court school in Aachen. Charlemagne summoned him. We can imagine the following conversation:

CHARLEMAGNE: Alcuin, I've got a problem.
ALCUIN: My lord?
CHARLEMAGNE: I want you to look into the mess in my Chancery. The clerks are unable to cope with the mail. They complain about the fancy scribblings we've been

receiving and I must admit that they are right. When a script looks like noodles drying on a clothes line with the wind blowing from all directions, it's time I put my foot down. Just drop whatever you are doing and try to invent some sensible hand. From now on, everybody writes the same way!

ALCUIN: Yes, my lord.

CHARLEMAGNE: And Alcuin . . . keep it simple, will you? Who knows, I might give it another try.

Alcuin of York was a well-travelled man. Anglo-Saxon in origin, he had spent some time at his bishopric in France before moving on to the Emperor's court at Aachen, where all the leading intellectuals of the time congregated. This is to say that Alcuin knew where to look for a suitable script.

In the course of the seventh and eighth centuries uncials had started to sprout long ascenders and descenders while their bodies shrunk. The style was

perfected in the famous calligraphic school at the St Martin's monastery in Tours. The *half-uncials*, as this hand is called, could have been mistaken for minuscules or lower case letters, but for the fact that minuscules had not yet been invented. All letters, large or small, were capitals. Alcuin was also familiar with the beautifully decorated Irish manuscripts which emphasized certain letters in the text. Putting the two together, he devised a truly modern script. For the first time in history, a clear distinction was made between majuscule and minuscule letters – or what we now call upper and lower case, or capitals and small letters. This was a major step in the evolution of lettering. It was also the last in the structural development of the alphabet. Future changes concerned only the style of writing, not the basic structure of the letters.

The Carolingian minuscule, as we call the result of Alcuin's efforts, was a success beyond all expectations. Charlemagne issued an edict that established it as the official script. The easy shapes and improved legibility spurred an interest in writing and, by exten-

The Carolingian minuscule, early ninth century

exuberib:caprarum.autouiumpaſ torummanupraeſſiſ.longalinea copioſilacaſeffluere!puer.ſur rexit incolomiſ.Noſobſtupefacti tantaereimiraculo.idquod ipſa cogebat ueritaſfatebamur.Non

Gothic versals, 12th–15th century

sion, in learning. All kinds of manuscripts were re-copied in this hand, including old Roman texts which would have otherwise been lost to posterity.

The early Middle Ages started the tradition of beautiful capitals. Called *versals* because in biblical texts they usually headed a verse, they called attention to the beginning of a chapter or to an important portion of the text. The Carolingian minuscule borrowed its capitals from the Romans or used uncials. Later, whole new sets of versals were developed, ranging from relatively simple letters to elaborate designs in which the letter became lost in a maze of decoration.

CHANGES IN STYLE

As the Middle Ages progressed, something odd happened to the minuscules. Slowly, their round bodies compressed and fractured as if enormous pressure had been applied from both sides. This type of lettering is internationally known as *textura*, but the English prefer the term *blackletter*. One look at a page of this very dense script makes the origin of the word clear to everyone.

Up to this point, the majuscules or capitals were styled separately from the minuscules. The blackletter was the first script to develop its own capitals. The perfectly regimented rows of this script had the appearance of print and, indeed, when Johannes Gutenberg invented printing (around 1450), black-

letter was adopted as the first printing type. It was to survive for centuries and become the most used type for the Bible.

Blackletter was eagerly embraced in all countries north of Alps. In Germany, where its angular shapes were in total harmony with the orderly Teutonic soul, it sprouted roots and established itself as part of the national cultural heritage. It was also much favoured in England, and 'Old English' is still an accepted alternative name for this style of lettering. It is very much in evidence in Britain, especially when one is looking for a pub. Bookshops, antique shops and, indeed, any business that wants to be associated with the 'Ye Olde England' feeling, cannot ignore this lettering style.

Blackletter, from a Bible printed by Gutenberg, circa 1455

fedos occiderut. Rex autem cu audisset iratus est: z missis exercicib3 suis pdi= dit homicidas illos · et ciuitate illog succendit. Tuc ait seruis suis . Nuptie quide parate sunt:sed qui inuitati erat

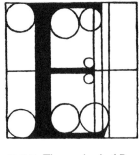

ABOVE *The revival of Roman capitals, early 16th century*

ABOVE *Humanist bookhand, 15th century*

ABOVE *Chancery hand, 16th century*

However, the southern Europeans never took to it and preferred rounder shapes. This was especially true of the Italians. While the Gothic was still in full swing elsewhere in Europe, the Italians were busy putting the final touches to a new style which became known as the Renaissance. During this period, under the influence of the intellectual movement known as humanism, architecture, art and decoration borrowed heavily from antiquity; so too did lettering.

Roman capitals were dusted off and redesigned with a scientific approach. Whole treatises on letter construction were written and illustrated by leading artists. The Carolingian minuscules, which some erroneously believed to be a Roman invention, were also polished to satisfy the new aesthetic standards. The resulting style is called the *humanist bookhand*.

Italics, the slanted lettering of simple elegance, originated in 15th-century Florence which at that time had a very high quota of artistic geniuses. It was also home to the celebrated calligraphic school founded by Niccolò Niccoli. Shortly afterwards, the pope Eugene IV expressed a desire for a rapid hand suitable for administrative tasks. The *lettera di brevi*, as the italic lettering was known, proved just what was needed and was adopted on the spot. From the pope's offices it spread into those of diplomats and merchants and, as it progressed, it changed names constantly. In English it is called the *chancery hand*.

Today we call 'italics' all simple slanted letters that are detached or semi-detached, as opposed to cursive writing in which letters are linked by connecting strokes. Modern italics are very much in favour with calligraphers, while printers use them gingerly because they do not read as well as upright letters. In their modern form italics project speed but they look a little vulnerable.

The technique of printing with movable type, invented in Mainz, in Germany, around 1450, could have been contained within that city for quite a long time if Mainz had not been sacked in 1462. Many of its inhabitants fled, among them the printers. Attracted by Italy's reputation for learning, they elected to settle there, most of them in Venice. Their hope for a golden future was at first squashed by the contempt with which their art was received. The Italians complained about everything. The blackletter was barbaric. The monotony of the printed characters offended their eyes, accustomed to the pleasurable individuality of free pen strokes. Besides, they said, why pay more for an ugly print than for an elegant manuscript?

With true German thoroughness, the printers set about adapting their technique to please the Italians. They did not make the mistake of imitating the spontaneity of writing. Instead, they chose to duplicate the Roman capitals chiselled in stone. The humanist minuscules received the same treatment. At last, their Italian customers were satisfied. From then on, printing became the leading force in lettering design.

CALLIGRAPHY VERSUS PRINTING

During the 17th century, calligraphers adopted a pointed flexible quill pen which was able to produce thick or thin strokes, depending on how much pressure was applied to its nibs. This resulted in very elegant swelling strokes, thin at the beginning, thick in the middle and thinning again towards the end. The script became more and more slanted and linked. This style is known as the *copperplate* because it was propagated by engravers who were able to make thinner lines than calligraphers. The calligraphers responded by exchanging the quill for a steel pen. The contest between the scribe and the engraver culmi-

151. *Italian hand. G. Bickham, 1743.*

152. *Round hand. G. Bickham, 1743.*

153. *Round text. G. Bickham, 1743.*

ABOVE *Formal script, 18th century*

RIGHT *19th century display alphabets*

nated in the 18th century with the *round hand* style, also known as the *formal script*. A simpler form based on the copperplate was the *commercial script*, used in business until the invention of the typewriter.

The art of beautiful writing was essential in all administrative careers and it was just as exceptional, then, to meet someone who had not been taught it at school as it is, today, to meet someone who has. I remember my grandfather's handsome writing, and I know that it helped him, at least at the beginning, to move upwards on the company's ladder. Although typewriters were already old news, it was still believed

that a clerk with a good 'hand' had the proper qualities for advancement.

While all this was happening to the written form of lettering, printing quietly developed in its own way. In the 17th and 18th centuries, some modestly decorated alphabets were designed. They all remained within the confines of good taste and the standard proportions were not tampered with.

Then in the 19th century a universal madness seized the world of letters. It was as if, suddenly, the door of a quiet house had been ripped open and a crowd of masked revellers stamped in. There were incredibly

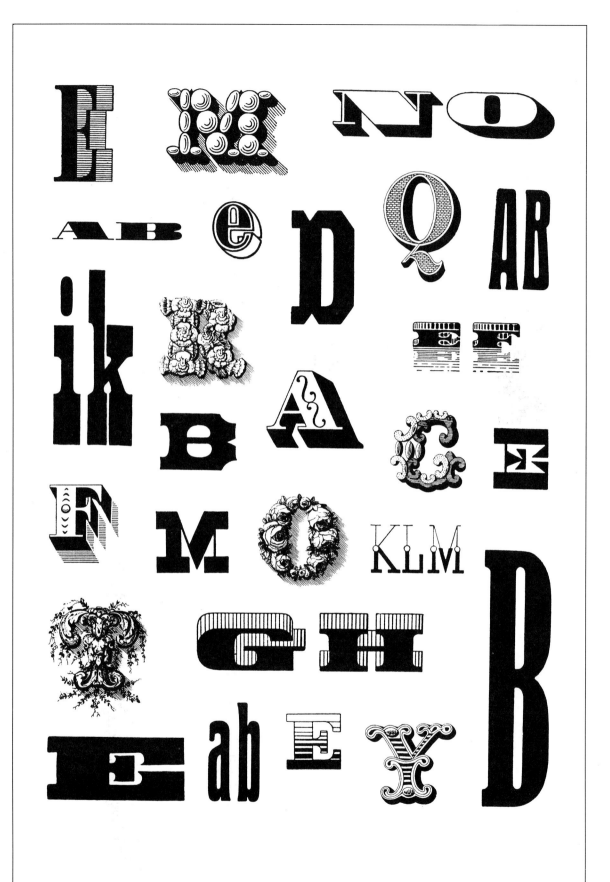

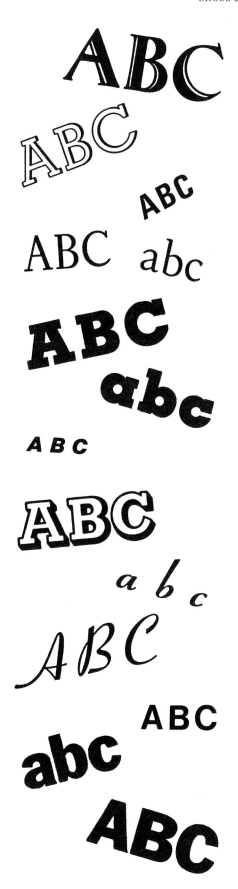

20th century lettering styles

fat letters and astonishingly tall ones. There were flat letters and three-dimensional ones. Others had grown massive serifs and looked like anorexics with heavy boots on. Some were made of bricks, some of pearls or seashells. Yet others were dressed from the waist down and shockingly naked above. Whatever their size, shape or decoration, they were all loud and boisterous, each calling attention to itself.

What caused this lunacy? Where was it initiated? The answer lies in England, with the impact of the industrial revolution. The advent of mass production and periodical problems in marketing started a wave of advertising. The subtle slogans that creep into the consumer's subconscious, 'image creation' and other sly methods of mind manipulation, were unknown to the Victorians. So, in the absence of other resources, Victorian ads had no choice but to fight each other for attention. They had to seize the potential customer by the lapels and shout in his face.

The variety of these display alphabets is such that historians have failed to classify them. In general they are referred to dismissively as 'the decadent letter forms of the 19th century'. However, while it is true that many of them were overdone and ugly, it is equally true that others had grace and a lasting value.

The 20th century has developed a simple taste in lettering, but does not hesitate to draw from the past if need be to create a special mood. Many of the modern types are recognizable by the absence of serifs. The *sans serif* system was developed as early as 1816, but in the ornamental craze of the 19th century it was treated as a poor relative. Rediscovered in the late 1920s in Germany, it became a symbol of modern expression.

Contemporary calligraphy has revised the main lettering styles of the past and, with the help of modern tools and materials, follows its own path toward new heights of perfection. Ironically, the art of beautiful handwriting is, once again, the privilege of a few talented individuals. This time not because the masses are illiterate, but because typewriters and word processors have eliminated the need for a good-looking, legible hand. For those who are not skilled in calligraphy, yet harbour the desire to create handsome letter shapes, there is a way: needle calligraphy.

THE WORLD OF SAMPLERS

ORIGIN AND PURPOSE

The history of Western samplers spans some 400 years. The word itself is derived from the French *exemplaire* which, in turn, descends from the Latin *exemplum*. The old English spelling made it into exemplar, exempler, suamplaire and, finally, sampler.

Samplers seem to have been born in the 16th century. No earlier pieces survive, but it is safe to assume that the practice of recording embroidery patterns on a piece of cloth is as old as embroidery itself. How could it be otherwise? In the absence of pattern books – none existed before the end of the 16th century – the only way to preserve an interesting pattern for future use was to record it with needle and thread.

The cloth, on which new techniques, patterns and colour combinations had been collected, was treated with respect and mentioned in wills and inventories. The oldest information on record dates from 1502, when Elizabeth of York paid eight pennies for a piece of linen cloth for a sampler. Seven years later, in 1509, an inventory of the Queen of Spain's household items reveals that Her Majesty owned a collection of 50 samplers, some worked in silk threads, others in gold.

Historians are often perplexed by the fact that so very few earlier samplers survived the passage of time, while many other embroideries made in that epoch, pieces that were actually worn or otherwise used, are still with us. One theory is that the Puritans should be held responsible for the wilful destruction of samplers, which they associated with the vices of idleness and vanity:

Fear God and learn woman's housewifery,
Not idle samplery or silken folly.
                              Thomas Miles, 1613

The truth is that the Puritans couldn't quite make up their mind where needlework was concerned, for other authors of the same creed advocated it as a means of promoting such virtues of feminity as industry, chastity and humility.

Actually, we don't even know for sure whether the earliest surviving samplers were made exclusively by women, as most of them are unsigned. In the past, embroidery was divided into a public craft and a domestic pastime. Professional embroiderers were almost always male. Through the Broderers' Company, which was granted a charter in 1561, they increasingly controlled every aspect of the trade. In 1609, an amendment to the company's by-laws prevented women from becoming apprentices and provided grounds for the prosecution of women as unlawful workers. Finally, the company grew too big for its boots and a judgement in 1710 put an end to its reign of terror. From then on, professional needlework became more and more a female occupation.

While men worked on ceremonial garments, banners, coats of arms, liveries or furniture upholstery, women of the upper and affluent middle classes applied their needles to clothing and small objects. At first, the art of embroidery was considered a useful and acceptable hobby, something to do in spare time which would have otherwise been wasted gossiping about the royal family. As the fashion for lavish embroidery grew in importance, so did the need to learn the art. In the 17th century, needlework, hitherto a usual but not obligatory part of a rich young girl's education, became the principal subject on the curriculum.

THE 17TH CENTURY: TEACHING THE ART OF THE NEEDLE

The new importance attached to embroidery influenced both the appearance and the purpose of the sampler. Up to this point, samplers had been worked by adults either as a means of becoming familiar with a new technique or, in the case of a professional worker, to provide a potential customer with a choice of patterns. They were nothing more than pieces of cloth with patches of patterns arranged in a haphazard way. Their utilitarian purpose is emphasized by the fact that some of the patterns are shown in the course of construction. As the sampler turned into a teaching tool for children, its layout became more regimented.

The material used for 17th-century samplers was mostly bleached or unbleached linen embroidered with silk threads. Touches of gold or silver thread, which hold a special appeal for embroiderers, were common at that time and continued in vogue till the end of 19th century.

The samplers were long and narrow with patterns running in neat horizontal bands. The width varied between 15 and 30 cm (6–12 in), and the length was three to five times more. Some historians argue that the width of samplers was influenced by the narrowness of the hand looms on which the cloth had been woven. Be that as it may, our ancestors were perfectly able to produce a fair-sized cloth, but they also hated waste of any kind. It is likely that the linen used for samplers was made especially for the purpose. The bands of cloth were rolled on to a wooden or ivory rod and stored in the sewing basket. As soon as an attractive new pattern became available, out came the sampler and the needle. Samplers made of several lengths of cloth pieced together are not uncommon.

Most 17th-century samplers are unsigned and undated because they were worked over a period of years. Signing and dating was introduced around 1630 as samplers became testing pieces for juvenile skill. Children were enrolled in sampler-making before they reached their teens. It is difficult to imagine a child of six or seven spending interminable hours bent over a sampler, but we are talking about the 17th century when children were dressed and treated as miniature adults and unquestioning obedience was considered their greatest virtue.

The 17th-century samplers feature a wealth of techniques. Besides geometrical patterns, decorative borders and motifs worked in a variety of stitches, there is also drawnwork, whitework and blackwork. As printed books started to make their appearance in rich households, their black and white illustrations served as a source of inspiration for embroidery designs. This explains why many embroideries were rendered in black thread.

Some samplers were worked entirely in cutwork, reticella and *punto in aria* (stitch in the air) – early lace-making techniques of Italian origin which were very much in vogue throughout Europe as a decoration for personal linen, especially collars and cuffs.

Although band samplers were the main form of sampler-making in the 17th century, the 'random' or 'spot' samplers continued to be made as well. As a matter of fact, it is difficult to date a sampler which does not carry the year of completion for the simple reason that styles of sampler-making overlapped each other and patterns were kept to be copied by subsequent generations of needle apprentices.

Rather than repeated patterns, the spot samplers of the 17th century collected horticultural and animal motifs. A period of relative peace and political stability made it possible to dispense with fortified dwellings. Houses were now built on open grounds which were turned into formal gardens. Gardening became a fashionable occupation and this, in turn, was reflected in the decorative arts. Flowers such as roses, daffodils, honeysuckle and, later, tulips, as well as fruit, berries, leaves and other motifs drawn from the garden were frequently embroidered side by side with birds, insects and animals.

Besides the naturalistic topics, embroidery continued to make use of traditional motifs whose history can be traced over the centuries. In the past, literacy was a privilege granted to very few. The Church and the secular authorities relied mainly on imagery to maintain their power over the populace. Images carrying symbolic meaning go back to prehistoric times. How consciously the symbols were used in decorative arts is difficult to ascertain: some may have lost their meaning or acquired a new one, others were used again and again simply because they were appealing to the eye.

One such recurring motif was the pomegranate, which once represented fertility. It originated in the Far East, but in European design it can be traced back to the eighth century. In Venice in the 12th and 13th century the pomegranate design appeared frequently on the much praised brocades exported to other countries. It was widely used in samplers and other embroidered objects – but whether it continued to have any significance of fertility is a matter for conjecture.

Religious symbols were abundant. A basket of fruit and a lily in a pot were traditionally associated with the Annunciation. A branch with a flower and a bud symbolized maternity in general and the Virgin and Child in particular. Adam and Eve under the Tree of Knowledge, the Easter Lamb representing Christ's sacrifice – all such images have endured the passage of time.

The motifs were usually embroidered in tent and cross stitch, which provided a hard-wearing surface suitable for items subject to everyday use, especially furniture upholstery.

THE 18TH CENTURY: THE GOLDEN AGE OF SAMPLERS

The traditional sampler, as we know it today, was fully developed in the 18th century. The use of the trailing stem bearing all kinds of flowers, fruits or leaves was extended until these motifs completely surrounded the embroidered rows of patterns. The ornate frame was born. The idea was such a hit that, since then, very few samplers have not featured one. Naturally, the addition of a frame completely altered the proportions of the sampler. The former narrow rectangle changed into something nearer a square. Furthermore, it was no longer hidden in the sewing basket. The new generation of samplers was intended for display: it became customary to sew a decorative silk ribbon around the edges and, sometimes, to fix a ribbon bow at each corner.

Samplers continued to be embroidered on a linen ground, but new materials were also introduced. A glazed gauze called 'Tiffany' was in use between 1720 and 1740, and a woollen canvas known as 'tammy cloth' appeared around 1780.

As for the design, the 18th century instilled more imagination into the samplers. Motifs and ornate borders continued to proliferate, but they were now subjected to calculated spacing. A central design emerged from this careful planning. This could be either a single scene or a symmetrical arrangement of different motifs; often it was a text. Biblical scenes were very much in use but secular topics, such as landscapes, courting scenes, family portraits, houses, pets and other familiar subjects dear to the sampler-worker, appeared more and more frequently.

The sampler thus became a picture rather than a collection of different embroidery techniques. Consequently, the more elaborate stitches disappeared completely. Some 18th-century samplers combine free embroidery with counted-thread, but cross stitch emerges triumphant. Its popularity was such that it came to be known as 'sampler stitch'.

Pastels and pale shades were favoured in the 18th century, both in fashionable clothing and in interior design. Samplers of the period reflect this taste in colour, which was carried on to the first decades of the next century.

Darning samplers However, a menial task was finding a place in the world of samplers. The act of mending a hole or a rent may seem unrelated to the noble art of embroidery, if it were not for the fact that in the 18th century darning developed into a highly sophisticated skill. It is therefore of little surprise that darning patterns were made into samplers with the addition of rich borders and pictorial motifs. The darns were worked by a counted-thread method with the material cut away underneath.

Map samplers The second half of the 18th century brought yet another innovation, the map sampler. The growing interest in travel found its echo in sampler making. Doubtless a map sampler was in theory an excellent way of becoming familiar with geography, although some of these maps are so inaccurate that they became a testimony to the poor education their creators had received.

On the other hand, there were very sophisticated maps embroidered over printed guidelines, which eliminated the possibility of errors. These maps were printed in black on white satin and surrounded by a floral design. The fashion for map samplers spanned some sixty years, approximately from 1770 to 1830.

Mourning samplers Another category of theme samplers born in the 18th century, and surviving into the 19th, was the mourning sampler. This was embroidered in memory of a deceased person: a family member or a dear friend. Mourning samplers usually depict gravestones, urns, mourners and the ever-present weeping willow, symbol of bereavement. The quality of the design ranges from a simple, naive rendering to a commissioned professional work. Mourning samplers were usually embroidered in silk on a silk or satin background.

While most mourning samplers briefly stated the name of the deceased, his or her age and the date of

BELOW *The Lord's Prayer beautifully stitched in silver thread and coloured silk on wool. The maker's name, Ann Clowser, and date, 1723, are worked into a devout dedication at the end of the main text (*Trustees of the Victoria & Albert Museum*).*

RIGHT *All the elements of the traditional sampler are included here. Note that this style of needlework was popular on both sides of the Atlantic in the 18th century (*American Museum in Britain*).*

death, all preceded by 'in memory of', some were more eloquent. One, obviously designed by a professional artist, depicts a praying nun in a church graveyard. The text on the tombstone reads:

Here lies the Body of
Mary Haselton
Born of Roman Catholic Parents
And Virtuously brought up
Who being in the Act of Prayer
Repeating Her Vespers
Was instantaneously killed by a flash of Lightning
August the 16th 1785
Aged 9 Years

An unusual tragedy that would have been long forgotten if it were not preserved with needle and thread. Poor little Mary Haselton on whom God played such a cruel joke!

THE 19TH CENTURY: FROM PEAK TO DECLINE

Samplers from the first decades of the 19th century retained the originality and spontaneity which were the hallmarks of sampler making in the preceding century. The central layout surrounded by a rich frame, established in the 18th century, now featured a lot of buildings. Architecture was not a new subject, but it gained in importance. The simplicity of the Georgian style made it possible for young embroiderers to include pictures of houses in their design. Family dwellings, churches and schools were now the focus of many samplers. The coarse canvas which appeared at the end of the 18th century made the task easier and more enjoyable, as it lent itself to the sharp angles of the subject and made the counting of threads less strenuous.

Family records, born at the end of the inventive 18th century, became very popular. Some were rather plain, with names and dates listed under a heading such as 'Family Record' or 'Family Register'. The majority retained the decorative style of samplers in which the genealogical information simply replaced the customary moralistic inscription. These samplers are, in their modest way, a poignant testimony of the frequent births and premature deaths that characterized family life in the past.

A major influence in 19th-century sampler making was 'Berlin wool work'. Although embroidery patterns were available, either as loose sheets or in the form of books, none were in colour until, in 1804, a German print seller hit upon the idea. The hand-coloured designs took the world by storm. Thousands were exported from Berlin, to other European countries and beyond. Countless people who did not care to decipher the old monochrome working charts were seduced by these attractive designs which were comparatively easy to duplicate. In addition, the agonizing over the choice of suitable colours which had previously been inevitable was now eliminated.

All this led to a surge of interest in sampler making. It became fashionable for adults to collect Berlin motifs and work them into samplers.

The world's longest sampler dates from this period. It was made between 1850 and 1870 by the family of the Reverend McDowell of Norfolk. Berlin motifs, worked on small patches of cloth by Mrs McDowell and her five daughters, were pieced together to form a sampler 12.5 metres (41 ft) long. Besides being a rarity because of its size, the sampler is also a silent witness to the deteriorating embroidery standards of the late 19th century. Fine workmanship and mellow colour schemes were progressively replaced by coarse stitches and garish colours.

Embroidery was not the only craft that suffered in this new industrial age. It is difficult for us, children of the 20th century, to understand the fascination and esteem the average Victorian held for machine-made objects. All of a sudden, everything could be produced faster, cheaper and, most amazing of all, with a precision no hand-made item could ever have achieved. Originality and individuality, the very qualities we praise in an object of worth, were perceived as flaws.

Late 19th-century samplers reflect this general decline in handicraft. Once again they were worked only by children and their main characteristic is lack of originality. The material used was coarse canvas and the newly introduced pierced paper. Many were embroidered with wool thread in bright colours. As wool is the preferred pasture for moths, 19th-century samplers are often in worse condition today than those made hundreds of years earlier.

As for design and layout, they varied very little. The *Dictionary of Needlework*, published in 1882, offers this 'recipe' for making a sampler:

Take some Mosaic Canvas of the finest make, and woven so that each thread is at an equal distance apart; cut this 18 inches wide and 20 inches long, and measure off a border all around of 4 inches. For the border, half an inch from the edge, draw out threads in a pattern to the depth of half an inch, and work over these with coloured silk; then work a conventional scroll in shades of several colours and in tent stitch to fill up the three remaining inches of the border. Divide the centre of the sampler into three sections. In the top section work a figure design. (In the old Samplers this was generally a sacred subject – such as Adam and Eve before the Tree of Knowledge.) In the centre section work an Alphabet in capital letters, and in the bottom an appropriate verse, the name of the worker, and the date.

READING OLD SAMPLERS: ALPHABETS AND INSCRIPTIONS

The earliest surviving samplers bear no alphabets, inscriptions, names or dates of completion. The only exception is Jane Bostocke's lovely sampler now housed in the Victoria and Albert Museum. She did all the above. Her sampler is dated 1598 and the brief text reads:

ALICE:LEE:WAS:BORNE:THE:23:OF:NOVEMBER:BE
ING:TUESDAY:IN:THE:AFTER:NOONE:1596

The private character of this simple inscription is miles apart from the moralistic verses of doubtful sincerity that were the standard fare of the samplers to come. We can speculate that Jane's sampler was made for her baby daughter either as a gift or as a part of the girl's future inheritance.

As samplers turned into testing pieces of young workers' proficiency with the needle, signing and dating became customary. Many children proudly in-cluded their age at the time of completion. It varies betwen seven and fourteen, rarely fifteen or older. To the delight of collectors, some samplers also bear the name of the school or the worker's dwelling place. One late 19th-century French sampler carries a full postal address!

As we have seen, the shape of alphabets and the style of lettering went through a never-ending process of developing and adjusting to new aesthetic standards in all domains, be it calligraphy, printing or the decorative arts. All, that is, except samplers. The alphabets in samplers stand frozen in time, the same letters appearing again and again for centuries.

In the beginning, sampler makers had a choice of two alphabets (the ones I have called Purcell and Monteverdi). In the 17th century, Monteverdi acquired a simple lower case and was used in this form well into the 19th century. In the second half of the 18th century there were some clumsy efforts aimed at embellishing the Purcell and Monteverdi capitals. At the same time appeared an alphabet composed of upright script capitals similar to those in our Rossini alphabet. The first slanted script (Haendel) turns up at the beginning of the 19th century.

It seems that, at that time, the spell which blocked the creative forces in sampler alphabets was, at last, broken. All of a sudden, there was a deluge of new intricate forms. Fancy alphabets, mostly composed of capitals, featured letters decorated with or entirely made up of flowers. Others were exercises in compli-cated geometric shapes. These alphabets were very much in accordance with the grotesque shapes of printed letters that characterized the Victorian taste (see page 17). In our collection, the Bach, Bizet and Mozart alphabets correspond to the late 19th-century style. Specimens of these alphabets are given later in the book, for you to use in your own needle calligra-phy. (See pages 67–89 and 114–138).

However, even in the late 19th century, Monteverdi continued to linger. One reason for its enduring presence is its simplicity. It is pleasing to look at and can be embroidered with a minimum of mistakes. For a barely educated girl, as most were in the past, embroidering rows upon rows of letters represented a

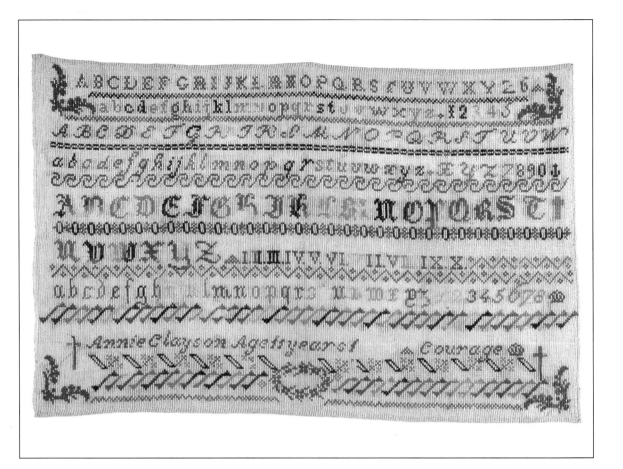

ABOVE *This late 18th-century English sampler concentrates more on the alphabets themselves than on the other typical decorative elements, but it remains a beautiful piece of work. It is Annie Clayson dated 1780 (Trustees of the Victoria & Albert Museum).*

LEFT *An English map sampler dating from the late 18th century (*Trustees of the Victoria & Albert Museum*).*

RIGHT *A sampler worked by Hannah Staples of Portland, Maine, in about 1795. It measures 54.5 by 40.5 cm (21¹/₂ by 16 in) and is embroided in silk on linen (collection of the Museum of American Folk Art, New York; gift of Louise and Mike Nevelson. 1978.31.25).*

debilitating task. Many of the poorer ones had never seen a book, let alone read one. Those of the wealthy families hardly fared better. Lucy Hutchinson, daughter of a Lieutenant of the Tower of London in the 17th century, complains in her memoir that books were locked away from her. Music, dancing and embroidery were considered suitable occupations for a rich girl, while reading, they feared, could put her health in danger. She goes on to say that she was allowed one hour after dinner in which to play and this hour was usually spent in clandestine reading.

Lucy was born in 1618, but the education of girls did not improve much over the next two centuries. One Boston boarding school, advertising in 1714, lists Writing and Arithmetics after such accomplishments as Filigree and Painting on Glass.

That sampler workers often had problems getting their lettering right is evident from many specimens. Letters frequently jump out of line; no distinction is made between capitals and lower case letters: they both inhabit the same word for no reason at all. Lower case y's are happily suspended in the air, the end of the descender touching the line; punctuation is omitted or found where it has no business to be. All in all, to these almost illiterate girls, letters were like little unruly animals which they found difficult to tame.

As the custom of including inscriptions developed in the 18th century, samplers became a reflection of contemporary thinking. Children were expected to obey their parents unconditionally. The easy camaraderie between parent and child, as we know it today, was simply unthinkable. As well as obeyed, parents had to be honoured. Any transgression of these rules was punishable both on Earth and, worse, in the afterlife. The fear of eternal damnation was instilled at an early age and reinforced for the rest of one's life. The following verses reflect the parent-child relationship, a combination of deference and search for approval:

Dear Mother I am young and cannot show
such work as I unto your goodnefs owe
Be pleased to smile on this my small endeavour
I'll strive to learn and be obedient ever

*   *

An emblem of love:
In this my parents Love doth show.
For learning they On me bestow.
Now let me learn My God to fear
And Love him with a heart sincere.

The next inscription may be a little complacent, but we can be reasonably sure that it earned parental approval all the same:

Mary Richardson Is My Name And With My
Needle I Did The Same And If My Skill Had Been
Better I Would Have Mended Every Letter
This Needle Work Of Mine Can Tell When A
Child Is Learned Well By My Parants I Was
Tought Not To Spend My Time For Nought

Although a worldly endeavour, samplers were a regular vehicle for religious verses. Quotations from the Bible, the Lord's Prayer or the Ten Commandments were embroidered frequently. Sometimes the religious thoughts popped up quite unexpectedly:

Julia Cran is my name
England is my nation
Lichfield is my dwelling place
And Christ is my salvation.

In other samplers the Lord's help was requested as the work progressed:

Jesus permit thy Gracious name to Stand
The first effort of an Infant hand
And whilst her Fingers on the canvas move
Engage her tender heart to seek thy love
With thy dear children let her have her part
And write these words thyself upon her heart

Doubts about one's worth as a Christian and the willingness to mend one's ways inspired the verse below. However, the fact that they are embroidered in the midst of courting scenes clearly indicates that the 15-year-old American girl had more pressing interests than working samplers:

If I Am Right Oh Teach My Heart
Still In The Right To Stay
If I Am Wrong Thy Grace Impart
To Find The Better Way.

The *mélange* of worldly pictures and pious words is typical of the 18th century. After all, it was an age where piety and virtue cohabited with loose morals. But inscriptions on samplers of the 18th and early 19th centuries are also laden with thoughts of death. To understand this morbid preoccupation, one has to realize that death was ever present. Child mortality was very high; so was the premature death of women of child-bearing age. Hygiene had no real meaning and the still insufficient medical knowledge was powerless in many ways. An amputation was more often than not fatal. Appendicitis, so easily dealt with nowadays, meant certain death. The verses dealing with death are blood-chilling:

There is an hour when I must die.
Nor can I tell how soon 'twill come.
A thousand children young as I
Are calld by death to hear their doom

*   *   *

And am I born to die
To lay this body down
And must my trembling spirit fly
Into a world unknown.

*   *   *

Then I'll not be proud of my youth or my beauty
Since both of them wither and fade;
But gain a good name by doing my duty:
This will scent like a rose when I'm dead.

Not only death but the transitory nature of youth and beauty were hammered into young heads. One couldn't smell a rose without inhaling the effluvia of decay:

How fair is the rose! what a beautiful flower!
In summer so fragrant and gay!
But the leaves are beginning to fade in an hour
And they wither and die in a day.

*   *   *

The fairest Flower will soon decay
Its fragrance loose and Splendid hue
So youth and beauty wear away
And vanish as the Morning due

*   *   *

Alas the brittle clay
That built our body first
And every month and every day
Tis mouldering back to dust

Fortunately, there was always the salvatory Virtue, practically the only thing the moralists allowed to last throughout eternity:

Virtue alone Can Never Die. but Lives to imortality
from haughty Looks Ill turn afide. & mortifie my Pride

Pride had no place in a woman's life. Humility and mediocrity came highly recommended:

Seek to be good but aim not to be great
A womanf nobleft ftation if retreat
Her faireft virtues fhy from public sight
Domeftic worth still shunf too strong a light

How sincere were all these verses? Were they deeply felt or just intended for display? It is difficult to enter the mind of the children whose hands embroidered the inscriptions, though the sincerity of this last text cannot be doubted:

Patty Polk did this and she hated every stitch
she did in it. She loves to read much more.

I wonder how many young girls felt the same without ever daring to say so?

SAMPLERS TODAY

In recent years, samplers have once again become a favourite subject for embroiderers. There isn't a thing a sampler cannot absorb: alphabets, motifs, borders, old saws, famous quotations; records of weddings, births, anniversaries, graduations and other family milestones. The sampler can cover all this and more.

LEFT *This Cottage Sampler contains all the traditional ingredients: an inscription, a picture, an alphabet, the worker's signature and the date in Latin, all surrounded with a rich frame. The chart for the alphabet, called Brahms, appears on page 72.*

The Cottage Sampler illustrated above is a typical example of an old-fashioned design. It contains all the ingredients a sampler in good standing should possess: a pious or morally edifying inscription, a picture, an alphabet, the name of the worker, the date and, finally, an ornate frame.

Even though the old-fashioned approach possesses undeniable charm, we should not feel compelled to create only traditional designs. Let's not repeat the mistakes of the late 19th century, when samplers became soulless exercises in stitching. Needlework is part of our cultural heritage and as such should reflect the epoch in which it is made. After all, past genera-

tions did not hesitate to include objects in everyday use, and people portrayed in historical samplers were dressed in the current fashion. I agree that cars, computers and mini-skirts are less charming than carriages, horses and crinolines. Yet they are part of our life. Future collectors will find them just as quaint and endearing as we find objects from the past.

LATIN FOR SAMPLER MAKERS

In the days when Latin was the language of scholars, 'signing' a sampler in Latin was a common practice. These few words and Roman numerals will help you join in this tradition.

Fecit (always follows the name) = Made by
Anno Domini = The Year of Our Lord
1993 = MCMXCIII, 1994 = MCMXCIV,
1995 = MCMXCV, 1996 = MCMXCVI,
1997 = MCMXCVII, 1998 = MCMXCVIII,
1999 = MCMXCIX, 2000 = MM, 2001 = MMI,
2002 = MMII, 2003 = MMIII, 2004 = MMIV,
2005 = MMV, 2006 = MMVI, 2007 = MMVII,
2008 = MMVIII, 2009 = MMIX, 2010 = MMX

BLACKWORK EMBROIDERY

Blackwork is a form of monochrome embroidery worked on an even-weave ground. As its name suggests, this technique traditionally used black thread, although blackwork patterns can be embroidered in any colour depending on your taste or on the requirements of the design. Black, however, provides the best contrast on a white background.

The designs are worked by simple stitches over a counted number of threads. The main characteristics of blackwork are small geometric motifs which are repeated over and over again to fill out a specific area. This area can be in the shape of a flower, a leaf, a fruit or another simple form. These shapes, in turn, may be joined into a larger design with stems or scrolls.

The overall look of blackwork embroidery is reminiscent of lace and one of the reasons for its popularity in the Tudor and early Jacobean times was that it was a substitute for lace on which there were heavy taxes.

THE ROOTS OF BLACKWORK

A good deal of what we know about the history of embroidery comes from official portraits of the nobility. With the help of art we can follow changing fashion trends, and the detailed work of the portraitists offers a vast field of study for today's needlecraft historians.

The great and the powerful wished to be portrayed in all their finery: woe betide the painter who omitted the smallest detail. A fine embroidered outfit was worth as much as an entire herd of cattle, so it was, indeed, a matter of some importance to show the wearer's wealth by faithfully registering the quality of the cloth and all the decorations that covered it.

Studying these portraits allows us to identify the different techniques of needlework in vogue at the time the pictures were painted. It also helps us to follow the spread of fashion geographically. Thus we can say confidently that blackwork was known throughout Europe in the 15th and 16th centuries, but that nowhere did it attain such popularity as in England after Catherine of Aragon arrived there from Spain.

Catherine came to England in 1501 to marry Arthur, the eldest son of Henry VII. The young man died a year

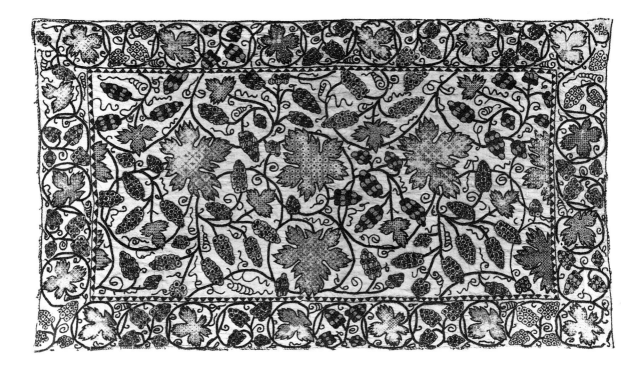

ABOVE *Classic blackwork. A 16th-century portrait of Mary Cornwallis by George Gower (*City of Manchester Art Galleries*).*

LEFT *Another example from the heyday of blackwork – a late 16th-century pillow cover worked in a grape pattern (*Trustees of the Victoria & Albert Museum*).*

later without consummating the marriage. She was then married to his brother Henry, the first of the famous Six Wives of Henry VIII.

To assume that Catherine of Aragon actually brought the technique of black on white embroidery to England would be an error, because, Geoffrey

LEFT *Blackwork doesn't have to be black. Any blackwork pattern can be enlivened by the addition of colour, as in this wedding record. It is worked in Smetana (see page 82 for chart) on an 18-count Aida canvas, using two strands of embroidery floss for the cross stitch and one strand for the blackwork. The result is attractively delicate* (Jacqui Hurst).

BOTTOM LEFT *The delightful alphabet in this blackwork sampler was rescued from a 19th-century French exemplaire. The alphabet is listed as Bach and the chart appears on pages 122–123. Diagrams for various blackwork patterns appear on pages 99–103.*

BOTTOM RIGHT *Out of fashion for centuries, blackwork made a short comeback in the 1920s and another in the 1960s, but is surely overdue for a revival. Aida cloth is the perfect support for its geometric shapes, which combine happily with cross-stitch techniques. Here, the blackwork in the portrait helped to create the illusion of an old lithograph.*

Chaucer mentions blackwork in his *Canterbury Tales* which were written at the end of the 14th century. The carpenter's wife Alison is described as being clad in a white smock with repeated embroidery on the collar: '. . . front and back, inside out; it was of silk and black.'

However, Catherine was a member of royalty and, as such, a trend-setter. We also tend to forget, in the rush of divorces and executions in which Henry VIII later indulged, that she was Queen of England for nearly 25 years – a long time to be in the public eye. Her liking for blackwork caused a wave of appreciation that was to last for over 100 years, and for much of that time it was known as 'Spanish work' in recognition of her influence. It is a historical fact that the Queen herself was a skilled needlewoman and her work was justly admired. She and her Spanish train also brought many

new embroidery patterns to England. Considering that most of today's Spain had been heavily influenced by the Islamic culture before Catherine's parents, Ferdinand and Isabella, reconquered the country in the name of Christianity, it is not surprising that many of the classic blackwork patterns echo Moorish decorative art.

Blackwork adorned many textile surfaces. It was used not only on clothing but also on soft furnishings such as curtains, bedspreads, pillows and tablecloths. In fashion, whole skirts, sleeves, male and female doublets, hats and coifs were covered with intricate blackwork embroidery. But blackwork was particularly popular for collars, ruffs and cuffs. These demanded the finest stitches and care in execution, for the pattern had to look identical on both sides.

In earlier times, underwear for both men and women consisted of a linen shirt, the collar and ruffs of which were visible under the outer garments and were therefore exposed to much wear and tear. Blackwork embroidery, decorating these parts of the shirt, not only served as an embellishment, it also strengthened the cloth.

The standards of hygiene in the 16th century were, of course, nowhere near ours. This is best illustrated by the famous statement of one of Queen Elizabeth's subjects, who writes in admiration: '. . . she batheth once a month whether she needeth it or not.' How extravagant, indeed! About 100 years later, the barber of Louis XIV of France respectfully implores the great Sun King to consider bathing more than just once a year because the dirt is so difficult to scrub off! While the grubby hands of the rich were hidden under perfumed gloves and body odour masked by liberally applied scents, the common people lived in blissful and undisguised filth until, and even beyond, the invention of modern plumbing. If underwear and household linen received some infrequent washing with still imperfect soap, the richly embroidered outer garments never did. Stains were dealt with by spot-cleaning, usually at home, although in the streets affluent citizens might be accosted by itinerant cleaners who, armed with flacons containing suspicious formulas, offered an 'instant and miracu-

lous' removal of stains. A third use of blackwork was therefore to camouflage accumulations of dirt.

All kinds of linens were used to support blackwork embroidery. The best were known as 'cambric' after the French city of Cambrai, and 'lawn', so called because it was first manufactured in Laon, also in France. The higher quality linens aged gracefully, growing smoother with each washing and acquiring a lustrous sheen in the process.

The black silk thread used in blackwork was manufactured in the Levant and imported to England via Holland. It goes without saying that these threads did not come cheap. Poorer folk preferred to buy undyed silk and then tried, with various degrees of success, to dye it black. The basis for home-made black dye was lye obtained from ashes, which was then mixed with walnut shells, elder bark and vitriol. This alarming concoction was not colour-fast and, worse, it gradually ate the fibre. Today, surviving embroideries often present blank spaces where there once had been black thread.

To relieve the tedium of black on white and to add a touch of luxury, some blackwork embroidery was enlivened by gold and silver threads. Metallic threads were made of fine silver wire coated with gold and flattened into strips, which were then wrapped round silk threads. At first the production of metal threads was in the hands of entrepreneurs, mostly women, but in 1622 the trade became regulated and forbidden to all except the members of the Company of Gold Wire Drawers. As with all trade corporations, this one was male-dominated and women were not welcome.

The term 'Spanish work' fell into disuse after about 1530 and was replaced by 'blackwork'. My guess is that nothing Spanish was popular in England after Spain had turned into a bitter enemy following Henry's scandalous treatment of Catherine. Blackwork embroidery remained common until about 1630. It faded away as a new fashion replaced the old one and lace became more readily available. Doubtless the embroiderers, tired of black and white, found more excitement in multi-coloured projects.

So great was its fall into oblivion that we hear practically nothing of blackwork until the 20th century.

There was a brief revival in the 1920s and '30s which favoured stiff, heavily outlined designs, very much in keeping with tradition. The second revival, which started in the '60s, has developed a totally new approach to the design. Modern blackwork has dispensed with outlines and is now used to explore tone variations by alternating patterns of different density. The patterns float freely over the canvas, often interrupting and overlapping each other.

Blackwork embroidery will never again attain the level of popularity it enjoyed in the 16th and early 17th centuries – there is not the same need for it – but it has a lot of potential for decorative needlework, simply because it is so eye-catching. It certainly adds interest to cross-stitch projects, and Aida cloth is ideally suited to it. The techniques and patterns of blackwork are examined in more detail on page 98.

It would be a great waste if the beautiful and intricate blackwork patterns remained forever black. As we can now buy lace without mortgaging the house, blackwork is no longer needed as a substitute. Instead, we can explore its use in another direction, namely by introducing colour. The idea is not new, but it has been rarely exploited. More is the pity. Personally, I'm all for it, even at the risk of offending the purists.

Initially, when I started working on this book, my aim was to create projects with just enough blackwork to add a new twist to the all too familiar cross stitch. As my work progressed I became increasingly seduced by blackwork and its endless possibilities. After completing a few projects I became convinced that multi-coloured blackwork was the right thing. The diary cover (page 108) and the tissue cases (page 112) are variations on the blackwork theme. The trouble is that this geometric embroidery, now vibrant with colour, no longer looks like blackwork. Actually, calling it multi-coloured blackwork sounds rather silly. A new term should be devised, shouldn't it?

RIGHT *The repetitive nature of blackwork motifs is well suited to any changes you may need to make in the size of a project. The blackwork area surrounding the central design can easily be enlarged or reduced to fit your tea tray.*

ELEMENTS OF
DESIGN

Lettering has always been subject to current trends. Like art, architecture and fashion, styles of lettering reflected the moral and aesthetic codes that prevailed at different epochs of history. The styles that survived the constant changes did so because, both consciously and subconsciously, we associate them with certain characteristics.

Among the people who know this best are designers of packaging. Have you ever wondered what made you choose between two similar and as yet untested products? Let's say that you have picked a slightly dearer one. Why? Something has appealed to you, something has told you that this particular product is perhaps better suited to your need or taste. As many labels are composed only of text, it is safe to say that the choice of letter forms has played a part in accomplishing this deed. A label on a jar of old-fashioned mustard must relay its message in an appropriate style. Had it been composed in a fancy modern alphabet its credibility would have suffered, no matter how authentic the content. Similarly, a 'hi-tech' product with uncials on the package would make you raise an eyebrow.

There is a multitude of other examples wherever you look. Take the enduring love affair between Roman capitals and financial institutions. Whether on buildings or letterheads, the Roman capitals say, 'We don't stand for nonsense. We are the most serious and dependable bank (insurance company, brokers' firm) and we've been here forever. In fact, if you care to believe that we've survived the fall of the Roman empire, that's just fine with us.'

As I was writing this, I received in the mail a religious pamphlet of some sort with the title composed of uncials. A very unsurprising choice of lettering indeed.

All but one of the alphabets in this book meet in this giant sampler for easy reference (the absent Britten – see page 69 – was a last minute addition). Compare the size and visual impact of the different alphabets when you are considering which to choose for your project. The random shadowing on the 'curtain' was achieved by using a variegated embroidery floss (Jacqui Hurst).

GENERAL INSTRUCTIONS
- Before you start work on any of the projects in this book, read the chapter on Materials and Techniques (page 91) and the Technical Information (page 142) carefully.
- The charts are drawn so that one square on a chart equals one square of Aida cloth or a two-square mesh of even-weave cloth.
- The numbers of colours refer to DMC six-strand embroidery floss. Anchor embroidery floss is equally suitable. Unless otherwise indicated, use three strands of floss and work in cross stitch.
- Before you begin, find the centre of your canvas either by folding it in two or by counting the squares. Mark the horizontal and vertical axes with running stitch. To transfer a design on to your canvas, follow the instructions on transferring design (page 55).
- Start embroidering in the top centre of your canvas and refer to the chart for guidance. One square on the chart equals one cross stitch.
- To iron, place the finished embroidery face down on a padded surface such as a folded blanket or terry towel, cover with a damp cloth and iron carefully. Remove masking tape before ironing.

Uncials have always been associated with the Christian faith. As we saw in the chapter on the Evolution of Lettering, their origin coincided with the spread of Christianity through Europe. Used in religious texts for about five centuries, they developed certain regional particularities. Perhaps the best known are the beautiful Celtic shapes of the eighth century. By extension, therefore, some uncials have a distinct Irish flavour. I would certainly use them for a St Patrick's Day design.

Let's stop here for a moment and have a look at the Music Composers sampler. It contains all the alphabets charted in this book, beginning on page 67, and spans a fair variety of lettering styles. I created many of these myself, and drew others from traditional sources, as we shall see. The idea was to have a range of styles to cope with every mood and occasion. Each alphabet has its individual characteristics and evokes a different mood. The elegant Vivaldi has less impact than the stout Verdi. The correct Schubert is a world apart from the cheerful, playful Berlin. The airy Sibelius lacks the action of Tchaikovsky and the speed of Saint-

⬛ 909	⬜ 318	⬛ 317	⬛ 310

⬛ 321

The choice of lettering styles and colours must harmonize with the text. Notice how the gentle Vivaldi script of 'Please' softens the brusque command, expressed in Rimsky-Korsakov. See pages 125 and 136–138 for the alphabet charts. (Jacqui Hurst).

Saëns. What then is the correct one for your design?

Try the following little test of your judgement. Suppose you have been given the task of designing four book covers. You are allowed to choose from four different alphabets, using each only once. How would you pair the alphabets with the titles?

1. Rachmaninoff   A. *The Manual of Competitive Swimming*

2. Vivaldi   B. *Mae West: The Hollywood Years*

3. Saint-Saëns   C. *Murder in the Monastery*

4. Wagner   D. *Evening at the Opera*

Compare your answers with those at the end of this chapter. If you have answered correctly, you have a good instinct or you know a lot about the subject.

The chapter on the Evolution of Western Lettering offers a short glimpse of the principal lettering styles and their place in history. Understanding the historical background of the alphabets is very important for anyone who designs with letters, and if you have not read that chapter I suggest that you do so now. No matter how good your instinct is, a solid basis of knowledge is always helpful.

As you will see from the projects in this book, the various alphabets are appropriate for specific purposes but would be quite wrong in different contexts. The No Smoking sign is a good example. Two completely different styles combine to form the design. The sleek, modern block letters of Rimsky-Korsakov are strict enough to express an order. There is no fooling around with this alphabet. The brusqueness is softened by the polite 'Please', rendered in the old-fashioned Vivaldi script. Instead of clashing, the two alphabets complement each other while expressing

different feelings. Try to imagine this sign the other way round, with the words 'No Smoking' worked in Vivaldi and 'Please' in Rimsky-Korsakov. Unconvincing and rather comical, don't you agree?

The style of the design, the message you want to convey and, of course, the size of your project will help you decide on the right alphabet. If you look at the Music Composers sampler, you will notice that certain alphabets, such as the ornate Bach and Bizet, catch your eye while others recede into the background. Don't let this fool you. The small, unassuming, all-purpose alphabets are the backbone of your future designs. First of all, size is an important factor. Unless you want to embroider a project the size of your living room, you simply cannot choose Ravel or Mozart as the principal vehicles for a lengthy text. Remember also that the eye soon tires of complicated shapes. These large, decorative alphabets are best for short texts or monograms.

There is another advantage to the plain alphabets: their neutrality. Britten, Buxtehude, Couperin, Offenbach or Ryba do not clash with any style. They will combine equally well with Haendel, Schubert, Rossini, Vivaldi, Brahms, Beethoven, Wagner, Bizet, Mozart, Purcell or Monteverdi for old-fashioned designs or with Debussy, Saint-Saëns, Sibelius, Tchaikovsky, Grieg or Rimsky-Korsakov for more modern ones.

Some of the alphabets are based on historical styles we discussed previously. You may have recognized Wagner as a blackletter, Smetana as uncials and Vivaldi as a formal script. Others are not so clear cut. Ravel and Janacek are a vaguely turn-of-the-century style while Rachmaninoff and Gershwin belong to the 1920s and '30s era. Two very special alphabets are Berlin and Mendelssohn. The first was created with nursery designs in mind but its awkward and rather comical shapes can serve as a touch of humour in 'adult' projects (though you may prefer to skip the flowers). As for Mendelssohn, which earnestly tries to imitate Hebrew characters, I hope that Jewish readers will be able to make a use of it.

Several alphabets in our collection form a select group of traditional embroidery lettering styles.

Monteverdi and Purcell are the oldest ones; they have been around forever. Haendel is also a classic, whereas Rossini is a composite of 18th century capitals – probably used in monogramming – to which I added a lower case. Bach, Bizet, Brahms and Vivaldi are authentic 19th-century alphabets.

A few words about the scripts. A script is composed of letters that are linked together. The capitals of the scripts (such as Haendel, Rossini, Vivaldi and. De Falla) were designed to start a word. They cannot – or shouldn't – be used to compose an entire word. Many beginners, seduced by the appealing shapes of script capitals, make this mistake but the result always looks amateurish. Please, do not do it.

Compared to traditional calligraphy, counted-thread embroidery is at a considerable disadvantage when trying to convey freehand pen strokes. Each oblique line is broken into segments the eye has to connect and compensate for. It is also impossible to imitate the slight slant of the old italics, although in the De Falla alphabet I have tried to suggest the slant with the shape of certain letters. However, there are aspects of needle calligraphy which more than compensate for these disadvantages. Counted-thread embroidery can borrow not only from handwritten styles but also from printing type. A judicious combination of both results in lively designs. By altering the width or height of the letters, by using different colours, different thicknesses of thread and other devices discussed under *Modification of alphabets* (page 42), you will multiply your options many times over.

It is now up to you to become more aware of different lettering styles and their potential. Do not draw your knowledge uniquely from this book. There is no shortage of material for you to study. Posters, book covers, record albums, labels, letterheads, logos, shop signs, advertising material, all this and more are readily available. Instead of glancing at them briefly, as you have always done, give them a close look. How many alphabets did the designer use? What style? What size, what colour? For what purpose? If, after a week of this exercise, you still haven't got a clue of what is appropriate for the design you want to create, take this book and use it to prop up that wobbly

table in your granny's bedroom. I can suggest this safely because I know it will not happen.

Before concluding this section, I owe you an apology. The moment I started working on this book, it became obvious that including a sampler containing all the alphabets would make it easy to compare and contrast them. However, I should have thought twice before making it an exercise in self-indulgence. As music is my passion, it seemed natural to choose famous composers as my points of reference. Unfortunately, I failed to acknowledge that most famous composers have the annoying habit of being foreign. So, here you are, stuck with all those unpronounceable names. Probably the worst is Janáček which reads YA-NAA-CZECH. Frankly, what was I thinking of?

MODIFICATION OF ALPHABETS

Practically every alphabet can be modified in some way. By altering the structure of letters, by elongating them or stretching them in width, by adding or removing serifs, we can obtain new forms and new styles. For instance, the rather old-fashioned Lehár acquired quite a modern look once stripped of its serifs (see the Motion Pillow project, page 108). Many of the alphabets in this book were born that way. All it takes is a sheet of graph/grid paper, a pencil and a rubber or eraser. Start with a simple letter and play with it, making it larger or smaller in any way you like. You will find that not all letters and all alphabets are equally submissive but you will end up with many interesting shapes.

On the other hand, there are ideas you cannot discover unless you practise with thread and needle. The diminutive Signature alphabet, charted below, would never have come into being if I had not sewn a wrong stitch. It split the threads of a square unit on my canvas and – *voilà* – there is the smallest alphabet in our collection.

Other interesting alterations can be achieved by using different thicknesses of thread and a variety of stitches. Instead of completely filling in the body of a letter, try outlining it. The letter takes up the same space, but has much less weight. Even the nature of the outline makes a difference. Cross stitch has a more substantial effect, back stitch gives a lighter touch.

For a three-dimensional look, try shading the letters. This is achieved by partial outlining. Shading can be added to either side of the letter, but it looks more natural on the right. In double shading both the right side and the bottom portion of a letter are outlined. Again, the thickness of the shading can be influenced by the stitch used. Depending upon how the letter is

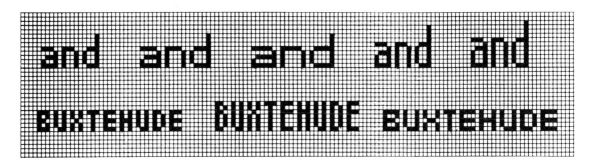

ABOVE *The modification of letter forms*   BELOW *The Signature alphabet*

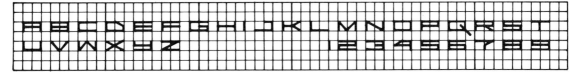

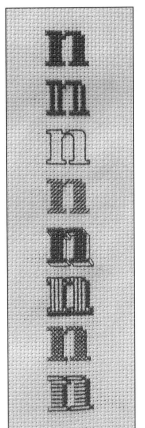
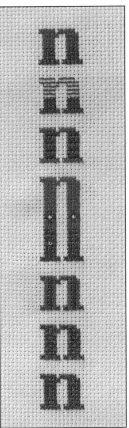

Varying the size of lettering adds another dimension to your message. In this case the result is both enticing and amusing.

You can make other interesting changes in letter forms by using different stitches or different thicknesses of thread, or by experimenting with outlining, shading and mixing colours.

filled in, we can use the same colour or a different one, possibly a darker shade of the original colour.

A variety of effects can be achieved with a single colour, as demonstrated in the sampler on the left. Observe how much lighter the colour is when the same stitch is worked with threads of different thicknesses (1 and 7) or with different stitches (1 and 4). If you employ two or more colours, the potential for various combinations is practically limitless.

Now try your own variations by combining the techniques from the two columns i.e. add shading to the multi-coloured letters or use threads of different thicknesses for each colour.

THE SIZE OF LETTERING

While the shape of the letters must harmonize with the nature of the text and the style of the illustration,

the size is influenced by the space available and by the importance of different segments of the text. Usually, large letters are reserved for the most important part of the text. In other words, if you want to emphasize something in your message, large letters are the most obvious way of doing it.

In the illustration on the previous page, this rule is completely reversed. Selecting a very small alphabet accomplished two things. First, the small letters are good for conveying the nature of whispering. Secondly, as when a good comic pauses before delivering the punch line, the message comes to a full stop at the most crucial moment. The reader's interest is aroused, but the eye must make an adjustment before it can go on.

If you were at some distance, wouldn't you take a step forward in order to learn what makes people believe anything?

Spacing

Wouldn't it be wonderful if all letters were about the same shape so that we could put them side by side at an equal distance and be done with it? Alas, the Latin alphabet is a series of odd shapes, some of which hate each other. (You will come to hate them too.) The most rebellious and disruptive is the letter L, followed closely by A, V and T, with P and Y not far behind.

Take the word CLASH, above. It looks just as bad as it sounds. Notice the big gap where the letters L and A meet. It becomes even worse when the letter A sports serifs. Since the strict regularity of the canvas does not allow for subtle shifts in spacing, what can be done, within the limits imposed by needle calligraphy, to equalize the spaces between letters?

If the word stands alone, the solution is easy. Simply allow more space between C and L and between S and H. In a body of text such treatment is impractical and unseemly. It would isolate the word and make it look more important than others: while avoiding one imbalance, we would create another one. It is far better to work in the opposite direction, drawing the letters closer together. Here, the bottom of the L and the left serif of the A were shortened. The letter S was brought so close that it now touches the A. The gaps still exist,

ABOVE *The white spaces between letters are as important as the letters themselves. Spacing should be adjusted to achieve a good visual balance, taking the individual shapes of the letters into consideration. With practice you will soon learn to recognize a well-balanced layout, because it will simply look 'right'.*

ABOVE AND OPPOSITE *A modern version of the traditional sampler. All the usual elements are there, but the geometric design and the mixture of letters from different alphabets give it a contemporary feel. Don't be afraid to use familiar objects in your designs – what seems ordinary to us may well be cherished by our descendants.*

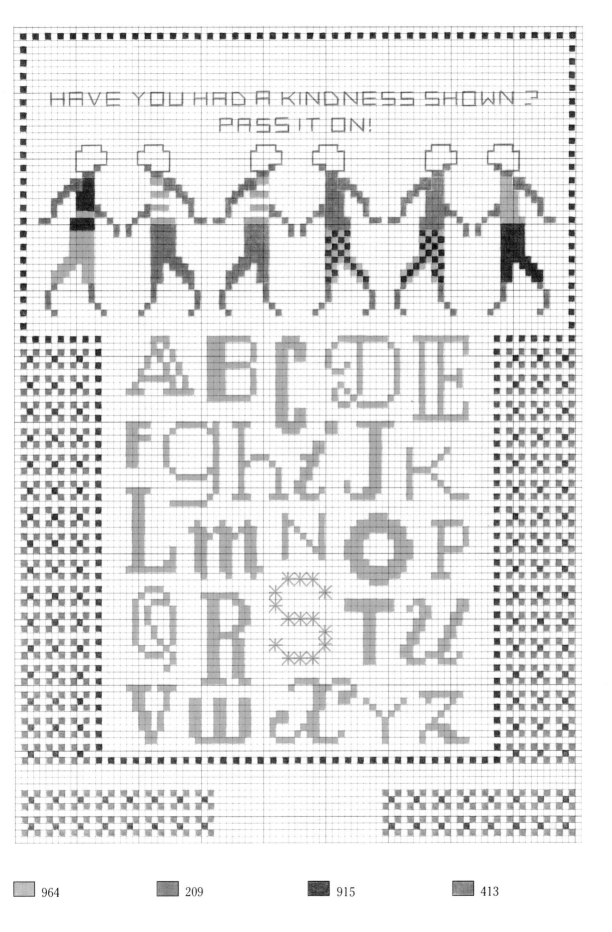

964   209   915   413

but the word is more compact. I admit that mutilating letters is not a nice thing to do, but such surgery is less noticeable than a disruption in spacing.

Sometimes we have to choose between two evils. This happened in the Tea Tray Cloth project (see page 37). The i's are too close to the other letters, but moving them even one square would have sawn the words into separate pieces. All this boils the problem down to a sort of a rule: when in doubt, closer is better.

This bathroom wall-hanging provides an example of incorrect spacing. The T bars are too long and the spacing between the two Es of TEETH is too narrow. Compare the photo with the chart to see what has been changed.

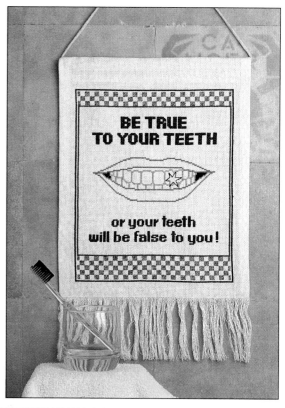

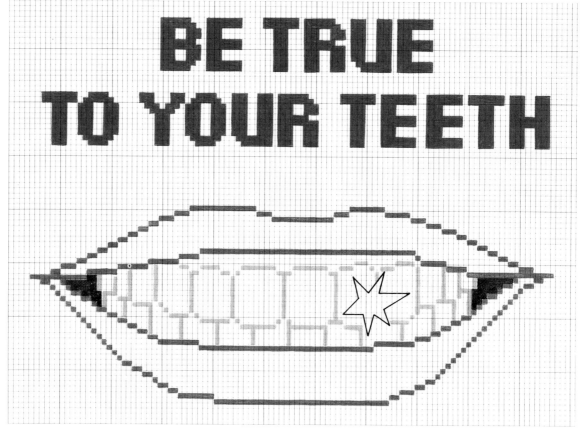

	3772		927		924		310

MARGINS AND FILLERS

A longer text looks better when both margins are neatly aligned. This is achieved by spacing between words. Normally, the correct spacing between words is the width of the letter 'o', but some subtle changes are acceptable. If the differences in length between lines are too great to be evened out by extra spacing between the words, we may consider using fillers. These are small meaningless symbols with no other purpose than that of stretching the length of a line (see the Agnus Dei project, page 49).

Since we write from left to right, we are used to a straight left margin while the right one is often ragged. The opposite seems unnatural. This should not prevent us from experimenting. In the Happy Birthday illustration below, the justification, as it is called, of the right-hand margin allows more space for a bold flourish and provides a better distribution of the massive capitals. Had these two letters been placed on top of one another, the design would have been too heavy on the left side.

ABOVE Any of these little devices can be used to fill an unwanted gap or to lengthen a short line.

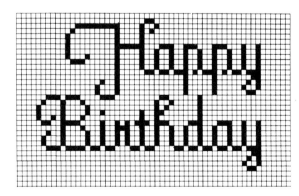

ABOVE Don't follow rules slavishly. Aligning text on the left is normal, but this design looks much better aligned on the right.

FRAMES

In most traditional designs, more or less elaborate borders are joined at the corners to form a frame around the central composition. Borders are composed of repeats, sequences of stitches which create a motif. The sequence is then 'repeated' over and over again to make the length of border or frame required. The size of the repeat greatly affects the adjustability of the frame. A repeat of 10 stitches offers a wider range of possibilities than a repeat of 20. It is therefore wise to plan your frame well ahead.

Joining the corners requires some effort in calculation and compensation. An unframed mirror will help

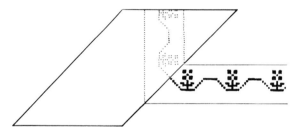

ABOVE An unframed mirror, held at a 45° angle, will instantly turn a border into a corner for a frame.

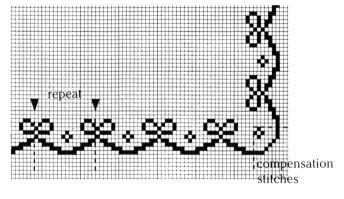

ABOVE Only rarely can a border be joined at the corners without some modification of the repeats. In this relatively simple frame, the corner treatment needed just a few compensation stitches. For a more complicated border, a new corner design must be devised (see the Cottage Sampler, page 30).

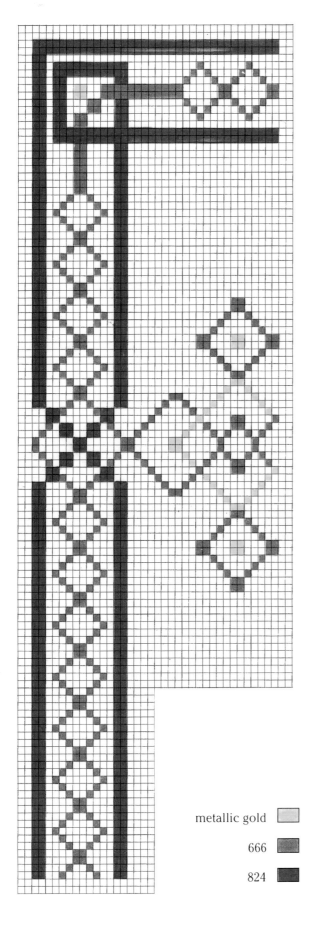

ABOVE *Here the lettering performs a double duty as text and frame. Only capitals can be used for this sort of design – lower case letters, with their ascenders and descenders, would create too much disturbance. This alphabet is Ravel (see page 134–135 for chart)* (Jacqui Hurst).

RIGHT *This project shows how little shifts in spacing between words and the addition of fillers can manoeuvre a text into a neatly aligned formation.*

The background to the picture is painted with fabric paint and the colour carefully matched with the red embroidery floss which surrounds it. It is practically imperceptible, and saves hours of tedious work (Jacqui Hurst).

metallic gold
666
824

you investigate different options. First, draw the border pattern on the graph/grid paper. Then hold the mirror vertically to the pattern at an angle of 45°. The two images – the real one and the reflection – will form a corner. Move the mirror slowly back and forth, as shown on the previous page, and you will discover different ways of joining the borders, either directly or with a slight modification of the motifs.

If you don't enjoy turning corners, there are other possibilities of border treatment, some of which are illustrated overleaf.

Finally, as in Love Makes Time Pass (see page 48), the lettering itself can become a frame. Capitals are better for this than lower case letters. The latter, with their ascenders and descenders, would give the frame a disjointed appearance.

MOTIFS

You may decide not to use motifs in your design, but if you do, select subjects that in some way contribute to the text by reinforcing its meaning. Hearts, flowers, birds and butterflies are favourites for illustrating poetry or romantic subjects. Houses, trees, people, cats and dogs, and more hearts adorn old-fashioned samplers. Abstract motifs are good for modern designs and contemporary quotations (see the Motion Pillow and the Purpose of Life projects, illustrated on pages 108 and 2).

Where do you look for inspiration? The projects in this book contain a number of motifs you can isolate and copy for your own purposes. For instance, the roses in the Tempus Fugit project (page 57) could be made into a frame for a text. Just extend the stems until they meet and you have a new motif. The sun and the moon in the same project could be used on their own in some other design. The same goes for the bouquets in Nature is the Art of God (page 53) and the Bakers'

LEFT AND RIGHT *Try your hand at some of these borders or devise your own to suit your design. Two or more borders can be combined to make a larger one. Explore different combinations and add your own elements – you'd be surprised how much difference a simple line above, below or on either side of a border can make.*

BELOW *Simple ways of using decorative borders*

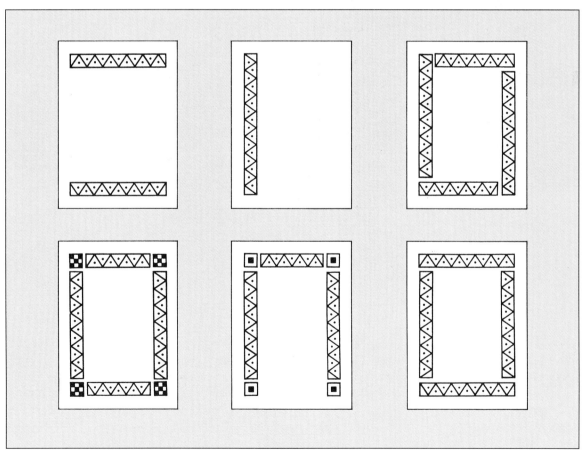

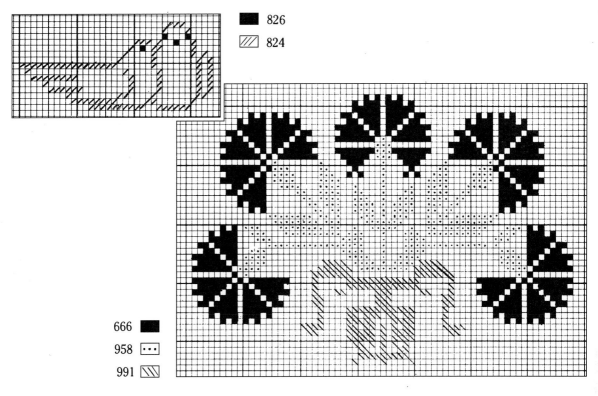

826

824

666

958

991

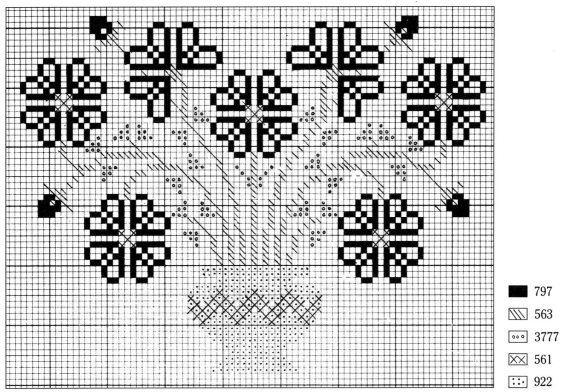

797

563

3777

561

922

These motifs are taken from the Deacon-Watson wedding sampler (page 34), the 'Nature is the Art of God' sampler (opposite) and the Bakers' anniversary record (page 63). They may help you when you design your own projects.

RIGHT *This traditional Transylvanian motif is complemented by antique Elizabethan alphabets, Monteverdi and Purcell (see page 71 and 119 for charts). A simple frame works best for this composition (Jacqui Hurst).*

■ 502		⊟ 310	
▨ Metallic gold		■ 333	
▨ 3608			

This sumptuous embroidery, glittering with glass beads, makes a wedding gift that will get a lot of exposure. The repetitive cross-stitch and darning pattern is suitable for albums of all sizes. The names of the bride or groom are worked in Rossini and the date in Britten (see pages 84 and 69 for charts). To make up, follow the instructions for making a book cover given on page 106.

wedding anniversary record (page 62). You could make a rich border by repeating the wreath on the Kerr-Brolly wedding album (below) over and over again. And so on.

Beyond this book there are numerous hobby magazines and other publications that will supply you with more motifs. Your public library is the best source of inspiration and there's no need to have misgivings about asking your librarian for advice. Most of them will be only too happy to help.

You may, of course, consider creating your own motifs. This is easier than you might think, and there are two ways to go about it. You can draw the motif on a sheet of graph/grid paper and convert it into a chart, or you can use transparent graph/grid paper.

To convert a motif, sketch it and, when you are happy with its shape, redraw it with a marker pen. Then, using a pencil, fill in the squares that are crossed by the drawn lines. See if the result is satisfactory. If not, make a change here and there until it is.

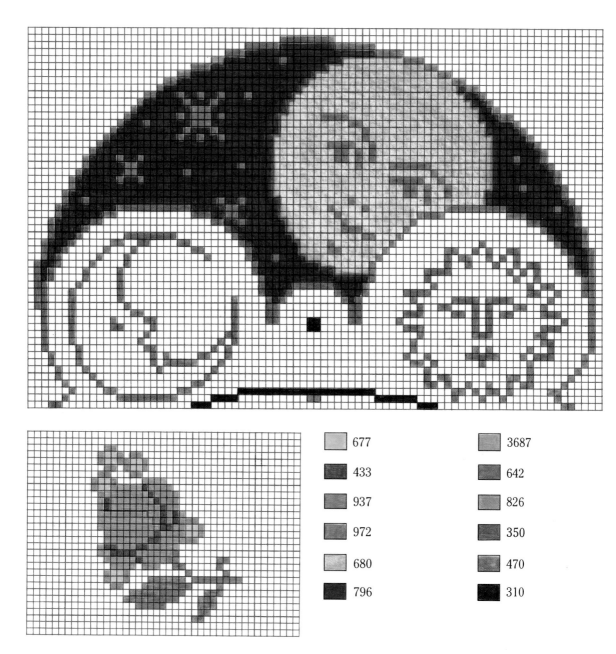

677			3687	
433			642	
937			826	
972			350	
680			470	
796			310	

Now you can transfer the design anywhere, using either the traditional counted-thread method or my new speedy technique explained on page 92.

To obtain transparent graph/grid paper, feed a photocopying machine with medium-weight tracing paper (obtainable at stationery or art shops) and photocopy normal graph/grid paper on to it. Place this paper on top of your chosen design and start tracing. The result will be a ready-charted design. Any interesting design from a book or magazine can also be enlarged or reduced with the help of a photocopying machine.

Use coloured pencils or marker pens to chart a painting or a colour photograph. You may need to do this in two stages: first, isolating patches of different colours and second, converting them into an exact number of squares. This is less difficult than it sounds and you will find that a bit of practice is worth more than a thousand words.

For the sake of variety, you may like to include some handwriting in your design. Look at the Your Smile greeting card (page 105), in which the style of the word 'Your' greatly enlivens what might otherwise be a dull design. The technique for converting handwriting is exactly the same as for converting drawings: if it's your

Time will never run out with this clock, although the Latin text warns that it might. Gold adds a touch of luxury to any embroidery, but don't overdo it – a little goes a long way (Jacqui Hurst).

ABOVE *Converting drawings into charts*

BELOW *Converting handwriting*

RIGHT *Motifs or illustrations should echo the text and reinforce its meaning. For this poem, hearts and flowers were an obvious choice* (Jacqui Hurst).

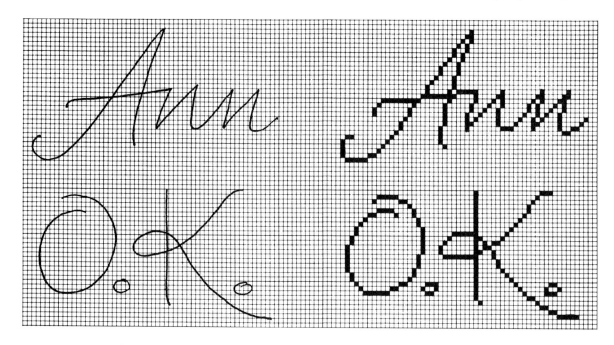

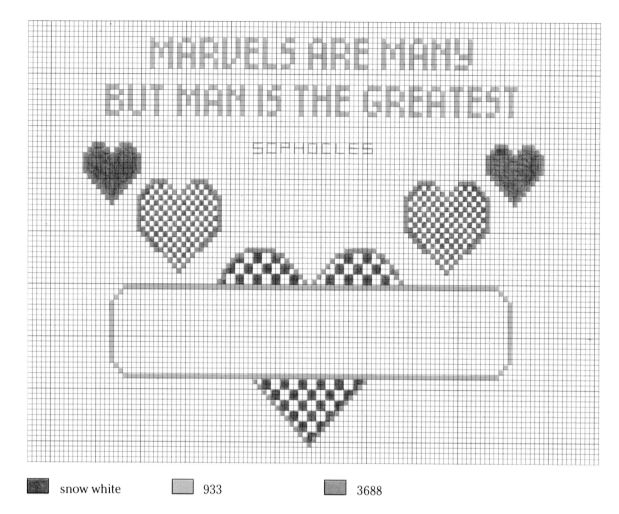

	snow white		933		3688

own handwriting you want to use, write directly on to the graph/grid paper; if you want to copy someone else's signature, use transparent graph/grid paper as described above.

COLOUR

Colour is a wide and fascinating subject, too vast to cover in detail in this book. All we can attempt here is a basic understanding of its use.

Probably the most important point to remember is that no colour is seen in isolation. Each colour is relative to those around it and is more or less affected by them. With this in mind, we must strive for harmony in our colour scheme. It is easy to be seduced by the different colours of Aida cloth available in craft shops. I urge you to think very seriously before you commit yourself to anything less neutral than white or black. The background is an integral part of your design and its colour cannot be discounted as unimportant. So, have a definite idea of your colour scheme before you buy this bright red or that dull green.

Start by asking yourself what mood you want to convey. Gaiety? Seriousness? Quietness? Action?

Tender feelings? If it is tenderness you want, opt for pastels. Gaiety is best portrayed by bright but not heavy colours. Quietness calls for delicate colours with a touch of grey. Seriousness prefers strong but subdued colours. As for action, choose harsh contrasting colours in their full strength.

A practical example of tenderness interpreted in colour is the Sir Walter Scott poem illustrated on page 59. The text is framed with a rainbow which is usually portrayed in radiant colours. Not this time. The pastels in the rainbow, repeated in the flowers below, create a soft, misty feeling and do not steal from the text. On the other hand, pastels would be a poor choice for an active project such as the Motion Pillow (see page 108). Here we want the colours to compete with each other, adding vibrations to the oscillating lines that form the frame. I chose a similar colour combination for the Agnus Dei project (page 49) which looks like a page from an old illuminated manuscript. Even today, hundreds of years later, these manuscripts conserve their wonderful brightness and, in this instance, the choice of colours was influenced by historical considerations.

MARVELS ARE MANY
BUT MAN IS THE GREATEST
SOPHOCLES

Sarah Elizabeth

daughter of
Rob and Marie Louise Haas

Born February 2d, 1989

If you are unsure about colour choice, seek inspiration in quilts, wall coverings, gift wrapping paper, upholstery fabric, draperies, pillows and other decorative items. The colours they use are always built around a scheme and most of them offer very appealing colour combinations.

LEFT AND RIGHT Birth records like this make delightful gifts. The frames can easily be enlarged or reduced to suit the baby's name. To determine the size of canvas, measure your design and add 7.5 cm (3 in) tolerance on each side.

Answers to the text on page 40: 1B, 2D, 3A, 4C

LAYOUT

THE BASIC PROCEDURE

Start with a rough sketch of your idea. Determine which elements you wish to include in your design – lettering, motifs, frame. Most traditional designs contain all three. Next, prioritize your copy. This means that you must decide what is the most important thought or information and give it due prominence. For instance, in the Bakers' wedding anniversary design the most important element was, naturally, the family name, so I chose large, bold lettering – in the alphabet I call Mozart. The second most important piece of information is the length of the union. Notice, though, that the line '50 golden years' is brought to our attention not by its size (another large or fancy alphabet would confuse the eye), but by the use of a different colour.

Contrast in shape and colour is essential to eye appeal. A good layout leads the eye quickly to the focal point. You may have noticed that although the illustration occupies half the allotted space, your eyes swept

Exploring Design
BELOW *With your preliminary sketch as a guide, assemble all the design elements before you start your composition. Chart the text in several alphabets. This will give you the opportunity to explore different possibilities while working out the visual balance of the design. For this wedding anniversary record a large bouquet, inspired by old samplers, serves as a motif. A large, old-fashioned alphabet (Mozart) puts the family name in focus.*

ABOVE *A preliminary sketch is the first step in any design*

BELOW *Prepare the background by drawing a vertical axis on a sheet of graph/grid paper. Centre the motif. Cut out the lines of the text and fold them in two. Arrange the text on the background and align the folds with the axis.*

ABOVE *As the previous composition seemed too crowded, the last two lines are replaced with smaller and simpler lettering. The result is still not satisfactory. Too many alphabets compete with each other.*

ABOVE RIGHT *This is a definite improvement. The design is more airy, more balanced.*

RIGHT *The final design is charted and surrounded by a simple frame. Given the limited colour range of marker pens available, the colouring of the chart is only approximate. The real colour scheme is plotted with embroidery floss. The line '50 golden years' suggests the use of gold, but metallic thread is at its best when used sparingly. The line will be embroidered in golden yellow with squares of gold here and there to add sparkle.*

over it and stopped at the line that says simply 'Baker', at the same time taking in the next most important information (50 golden years).

When the design and its proportions are clearly established – you will probably need more than one sketch before you arrive at this stage – proceed with the charting and the final layout. At this point you must decide whether to plan the layout from the inside out or the outside in. If you intend to use an elaborate frame or if you are limited to a specific size, it is best to start on the outside and work your way in. Naturally, all the dimensions within the frame, such as the size of lettering and the spacing, will be subject to the limitations established by the format. However, if you do not have to worry about the finished size of your project, start in the centre and add the frame later.

Next, prepare the background for your design. Graph/grid paper in various 'counts' is available from stationers and art shops. (The count is the number of squares to the inch or centimetre.) In Britain it is sold in both metric and imperial form, but as the 'count' of Aida cloth is measured in squares to the inch (see

page 92), buying graph/grid paper that works in inches will make your life easier. Try to match the size of squares on your paper with those on the canvas you intend to use. This way your chart will be the same size as your embroidery, an advantage if you have to control the size of your design.

Make sure you have a plentiful supply of your chosen graph/grid paper. You will need at least one sheet for the background (if your project is large you

If the width of the design totals an even number of squares, the vertical axis is formed by a line between squares. If the total is an odd number, the centre is a square.

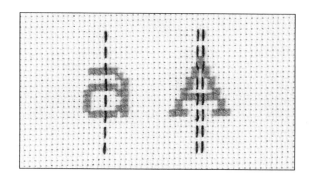

64

may have to piece together two or more sheets) and another for charting the lettering and motifs, which you will then cut out and arrange on the background. You will probably want to introduce some changes in the design and experiment with different alphabets before you are satisfied, so spare sheets of graph/grid paper may be useful. You will also need a sharp pencil (preferably the ever-sharp variety), a soft rubber or eraser, coloured marker pens, scissors and a supply of masking tape.

With a pencil, chart the elements of your design on the graph/grid paper, as described on page 55. That is, fill in the prescribed number of squares, referring constantly to the alphabet or motif you want to copy. When you have finished, cut out these little charts and find their vertical axis (the 'line' running from top to bottom through the centre of the design) either by counting the squares or by folding the charts in half. You will notice that if the width of a charted design totals an odd number of squares, the vertical axis is a square, and if it is an even number, the axis is formed by a line between two squares.

If you plan a symmetrical design, the nature of the vertical axis is of great importance. Should it be a square or a line between squares? The decision will be influenced by the count of the most important elements. For instance, if the width of the focal point (such as the name 'Baker' in the Golden Wedding design we looked at on page 63) consists of an odd number of squares or if the decorative frame is based on an odd repeat (most of them are), then opt for a square as the vertical axis for the rest of your design, too. Try to reduce the width of the other elements to an odd number of squares. This should not pose a problem when dealing with a line of text where a square can be added or subtracted by adjusting the spacing between words.

Mark the vertical axis in the centre of the background sheet and add a horizontal axis so that the background is now divided into four equal parts. Take your cut-outs and distribute them over the sheet. Rearrange them as often as you like until you find the best position for each of them. In a symmetrical design, centre each element along the vertical axis.

When you think you have found the right position for each cut-out, use tiny pieces of masking tape to hold them in place.

Now tape the finished product on a wall, sit down and study the composition. This is the most important step in your creative process. First of all, squint. By deliberately blurring your vision you will be able to take in all the forms as a compact unit. Is the focal point well defined? Is the weight of the design well distributed? Or are some portions too crowded while elsewhere elements float around with too much space between them? Is the layout well balanced or is it too heavy on one side? More likely than not you will find several imperfections. You may even decide on a radical change in the design. Act on your decision and repeat the process.

Once you are completely satisfied, use your marker pens to work in the colour. As mentioned earlier, the choice of colour may add a new focal point to your design. In some instances it may be the only one. In a text using only one alphabet in one size, a word or a line in a different colour immediately attracts attention. Again, study the composition at a distance to determine whether you have achieved the right effect.

When both the layout and the colour choice are as perfect as you can make them, it is time to chart them permanently on to the background. Impatient natures may want to skip this step, but I strongly advise against it. We are dealing with an uncompromising medium where every little square counts, and errors are much easier to correct on a chart than on the canvas. It is better to spend the additional time making sure things are right and clear from the beginning.

Prepare a new background for the final chart. Mark the vertical and horizontal axes. By counting squares from the centre, find the position for each element which you have established on the first chart. Draw each element accurately in position with a pencil and when you have finished examine the new chart for possible mistakes and last-minute adjustments. Then colour the pencilled areas in with coloured marker pens. When the ink is dry, erase the pencil marks. Except for the grid, this final working chart should be the exact image of the finished embroidery.

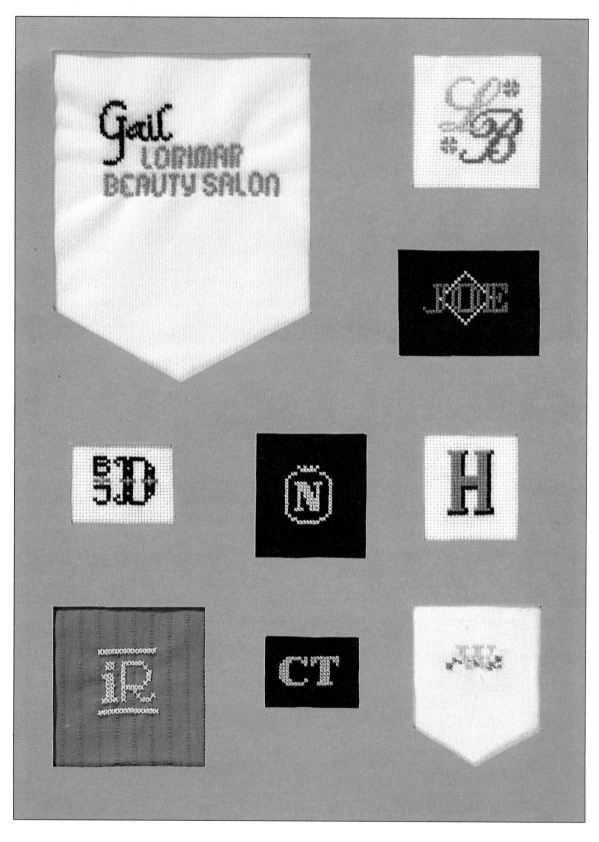

Experiment with letter forms when you are working on monograms and you will find that you can produce an enormous variety of styles. The wasted canvas technique (see page 95) is ideal for embroidering monograms on garments and material that doesn't have an obvious weave.

THE ALPHABETS

For the sake of simplicity, most of the alphabets which appear on the next 24 pages, and which continue on page 114, have been drawn to fit a standard grid. If you wish to make an alphabet larger or smaller to suit an individual project, you can use a larger or smaller weave canvas. But remember that the tiny alphabets were designed to be tiny and the big, bold ones to be big and bold – they may not 'work' if you distort them too much.

MAHLER

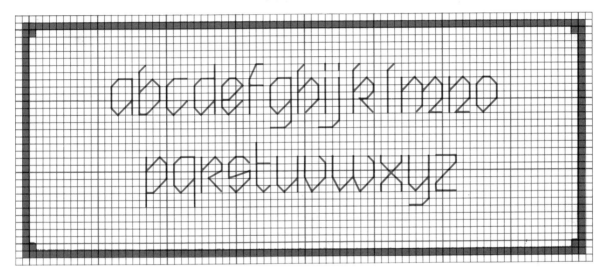

RYBA

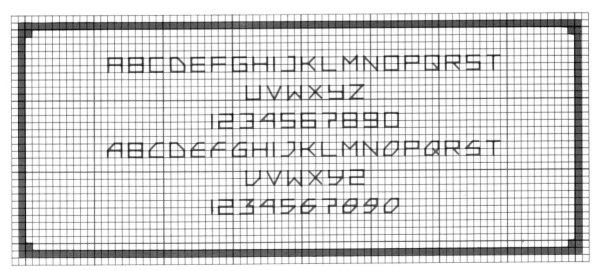

RACHMANINOFF

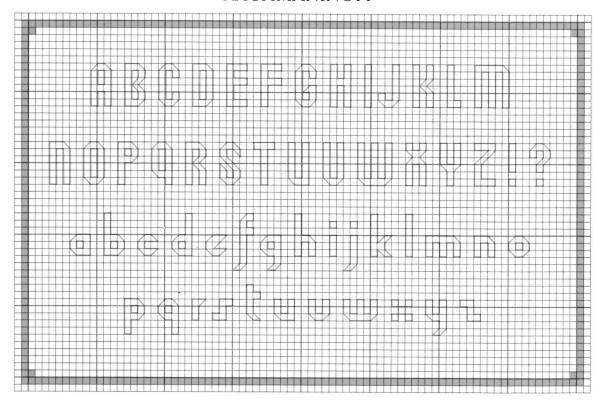

DELIBES

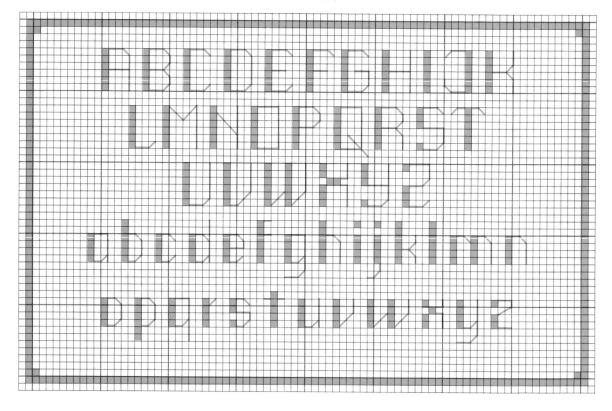

BUXTEHUDE

BRITTEN

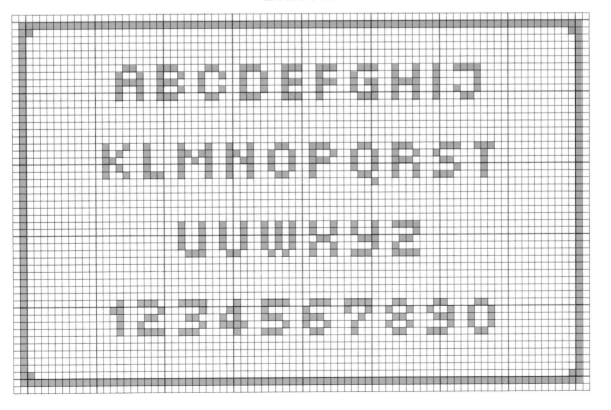

LEONCAVALLO

OFFENBACH

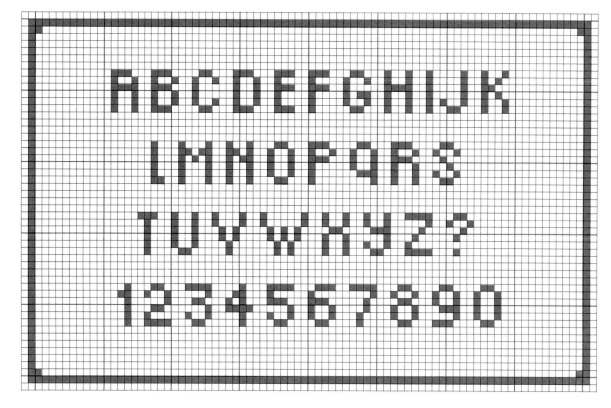

SAINT-SAENS

MONTEVERDI

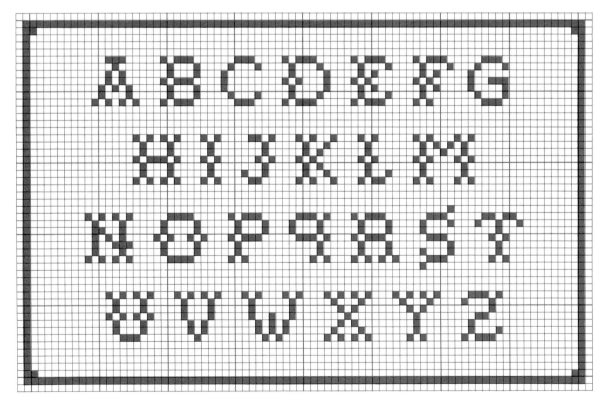

BRAHMS

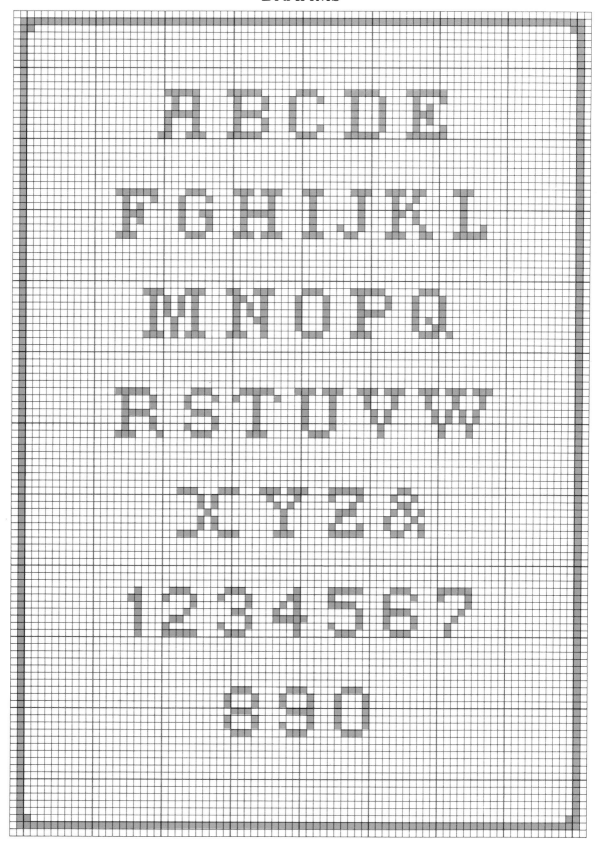

GLINKA

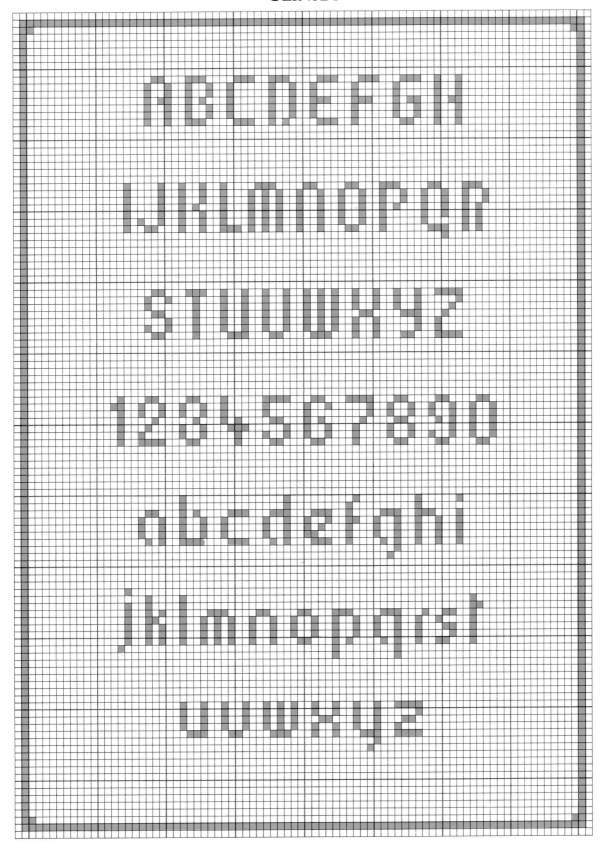

MUSIC

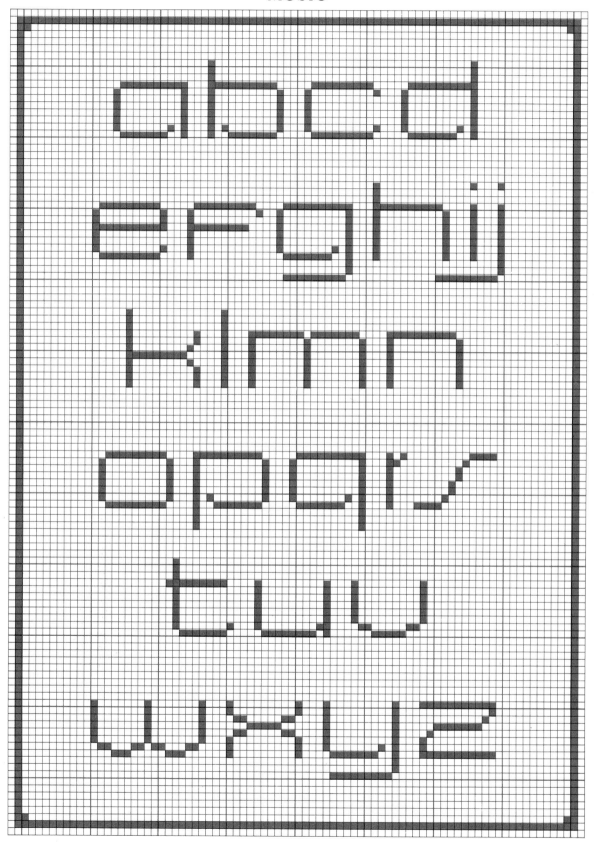

COUPERIN

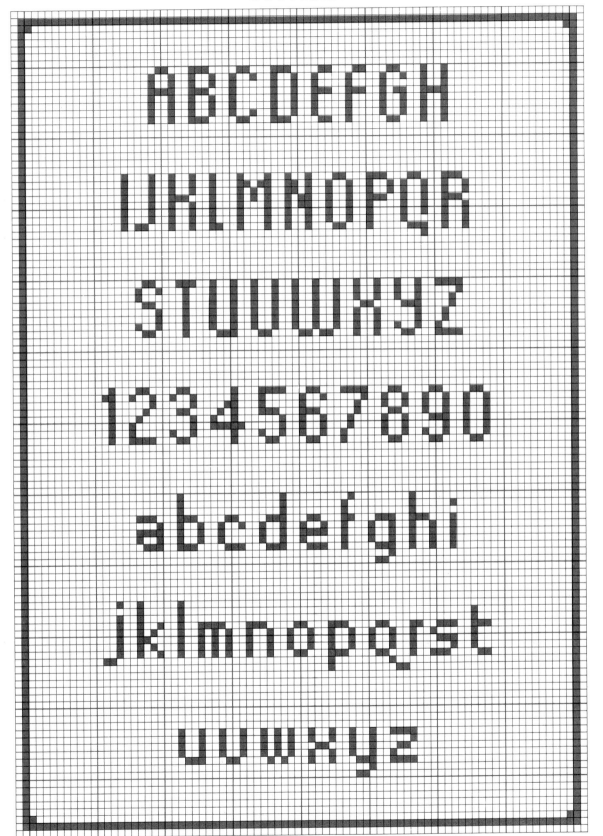

HAENDEL

LEHÁR

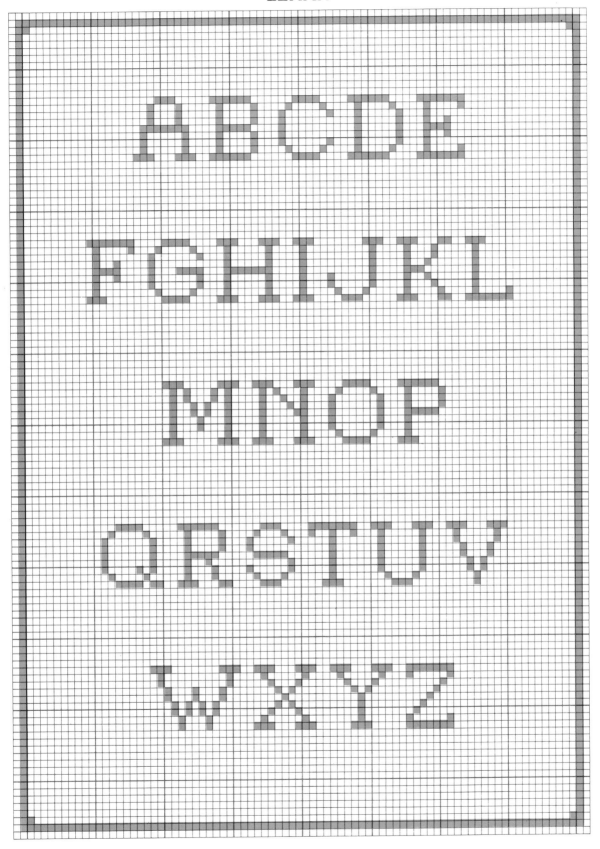

BERLIOZ

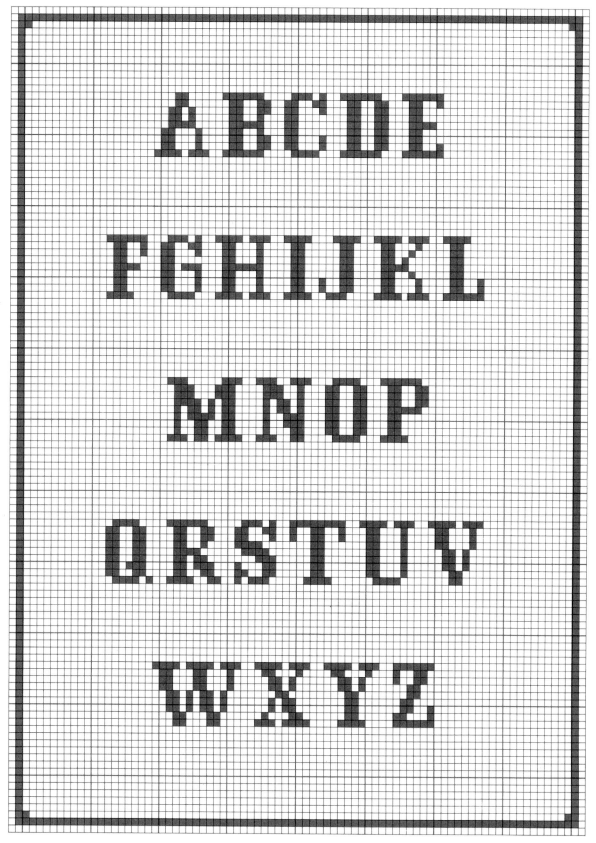

PUCCINI

BEETHOVEN

JANÁCEK

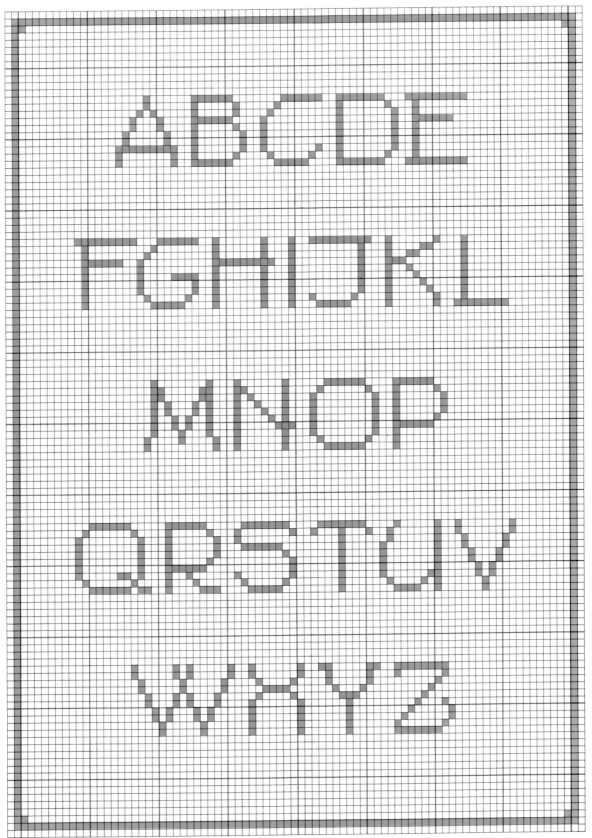

SMETANA

DEBUSSY

ROSSINI

MENDELSSOHN

DE FALLA

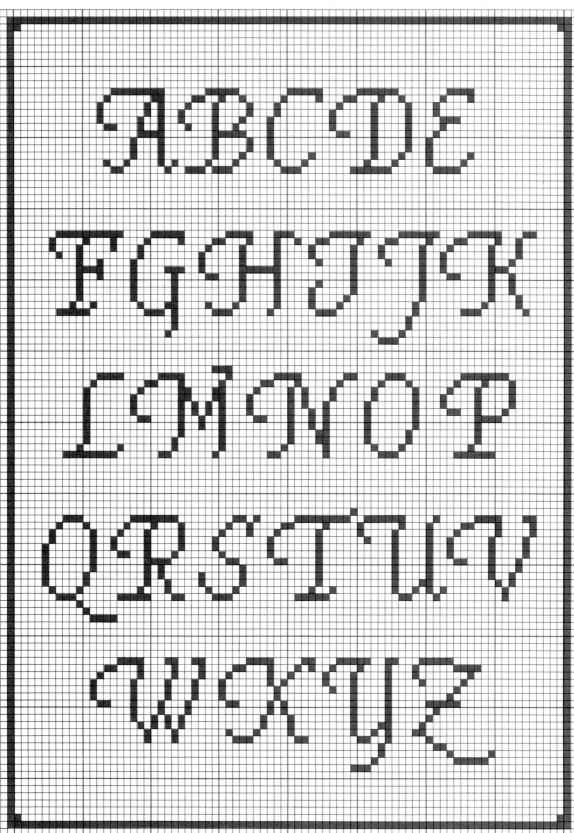

DE FALLA

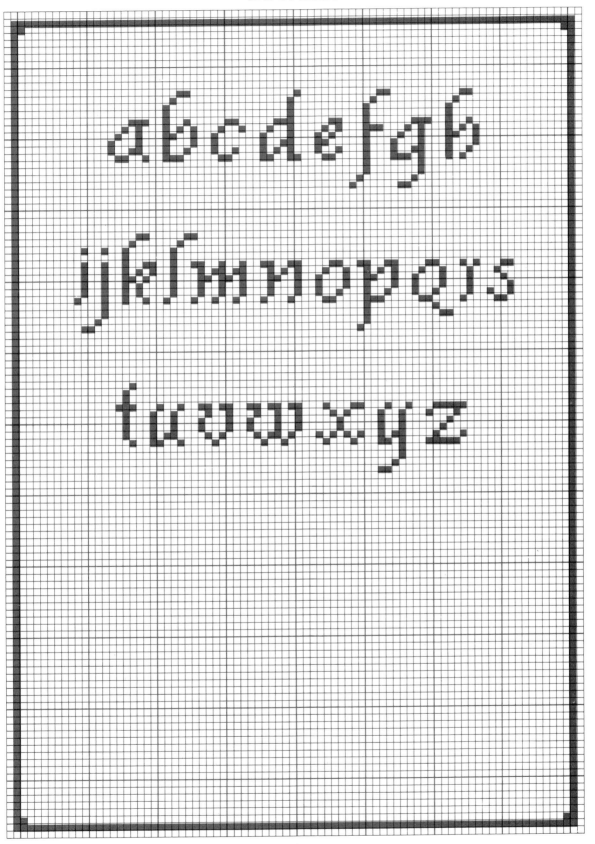

GOUNOD

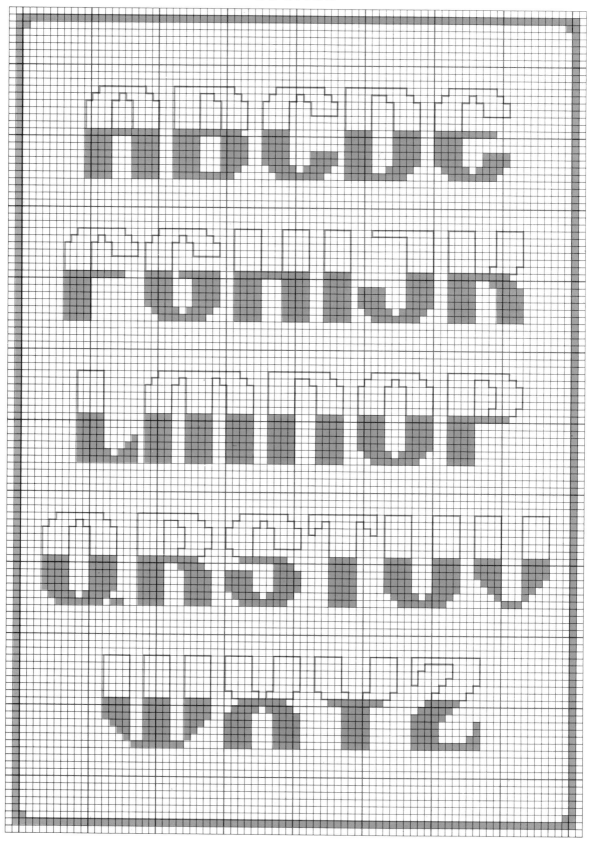

SCHUBERT

more alphabets on page 114

Materials
and Techniques

Aida cloth

Aida cloth is a canvas especially manufactured for cross stitching, but it can be also used for blackwork and other counted-thread techniques. It is woven in a variation of basketweave which locks groups of threads in even squares. This produces small holes at the corners of each square, and the needle is introduced through these holes. Sturdy and easy to

Different counts of Aida cloth

LEFT *Aida cloth with its woven-in pattern provides a ready-made frame. The simple message is worked in no-nonsense Verdi (see page 127).*

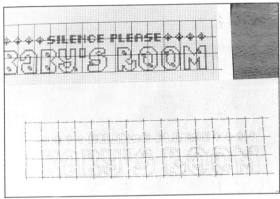

Transferring design

ABOVE *The completed design was divided into 10 by 10 squares. The same number of squares were stitched on the canvas with long running stitch, using a black sewing thread. The design was then transferred, square by square, on to the canvas.*

When the threads are removed, the canvas is ready for embroidery.

BELOW *The finished work.*

embroider, Aida cloth provides the best support for counted-thread needlework and helps make stitches look neat and even.

Aida comes in a variety of colours and counts. A count represents the number of squares to the inch (2.5 cm). Thus a 6-count Aida has six squares to the inch. Other counts available are 8, 11, 14, 18 and 22, with the 14-count being the standard size for most cross-stitch projects.

It is not essential to use Aida cloth for needle calligraphy, although I do recommend it, particularly if you are a beginner. Whatever fabric you use in your projects, make sure that it is an even-weave one which consists of the same number and thickness of warp and weft threads. An uneven weave would distort the design and spoil the effect.

To determine whether a fabric is truly an even weave, embroider a square of at least five by five cross stitches and measure it. If the vertical and horizontal sides are of the same length, then the fabric is suitable.

A NEW TECHNIQUE

Thanks to Aida cloth I was able to develop a speedy new technique which enabled me to complete all the projects in this book within the incredibly short span of 18 months. It is now possible to avoid the drudgery of constantly following the chart while working. Instead, the design is transferred to the fabric, leaving you free to talk, listen to music or just daydream without the slightest danger of mistakes. You refer to the chart only as a colour guide. You can also complete one colour at a time, which represents a great economy of time and thread.

However, if you are willing to forgo the above benefits for the pleasure of piecing your project together like a puzzle, there is nothing to prevent you working in the traditional way of counting stitches as you go. It is a time-consuming technique suitable for patient souls, but we all have to fall back on it when using other support than Aida cloth.

Whether you are results-orientated, eager to learn something new or just curious, follow me through the next few steps. For the sake of brevity, from now on I will refer to Aida cloth simply as canvas.

PREPARING THE CANVAS

After completing your layout, as described in the previous chapter, count the total number of squares lengthwise and widthwise. Let's say that your total is 140 by 112. Your task now is to convert squares to inches (units of 2.5 cm). If you have chosen the 14-count canvas, divide 140 and 112 by 14: your design will measure 10 by 8 in (25 by 20 cm). Too small? Use a lesser count Aida, say 8 or 11 stitches to the inch (2.5 cm). Because you get fewer stitches to the inch (2.5 cm), the design becomes larger. If 10 by 8 in (25 by 20 cm) is too large, using 18- or 22-count Aida will reduce the size considerably.

Once you have determined the length and width of the finished project, you must add tolerance. This is the unworked space that surrounds the design. For small projects such as greeting cards, 2.5 cm (1 in) on each side is all you need. Medium-sized and large projects will require about 7.5 cm (3 in) on each side. Let's go back to the example above: in order to accommodate a 25 by 20 cm (10 by 8 in) design, you will need a 40 by 35 cm (16 by 14 in) canvas – that is 25 + 7.5 + 7.5 cm by 20 + 7.5 + 7.5 cm or 10 + 3 + 3 in by 8 + 3 + 3 in.

Canvas is normally available only in one or two standard widths and you buy a specified length cut from a roll – just like dressmaking fabric. So you will probably have to cut your canvas to the correct size. Do not use your sewing scissors for this purpose, or you will blunt them in no time.

The next step is to secure the edges of the canvas to prevent fraying. This is best done with masking tape, but you can also use fabric glue, sold especially for this purpose in needlework shops, or turn the edges of the canvas under and oversew them.
Important: do not pre-shrink Aida cloth.

TRANSFERRING A DESIGN TO CANVAS

Using a coloured sewing thread and running stitch, divide the canvas into blocks of ten squares by ten. Choose a ten-by-ten square on your chart and find a corresponding square on the canvas. With a very sharp pencil, draw the required number of stitches in the square, running the pencil from hole to hole and counting as you go. When this square is completed, go

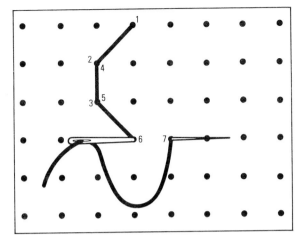

Back Stitch

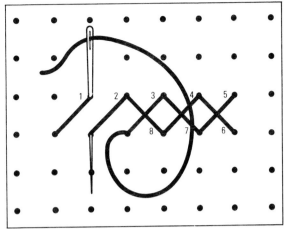

Cross stitch

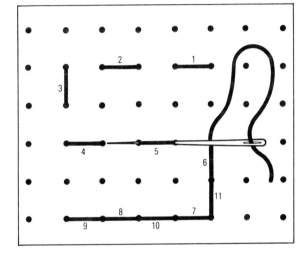

Algerian eye stitch

Double running stitch

on to the next one until you have covered the whole design. Press very lightly and work slowly – it is worth taking the extra time to avoid mistakes. If, in spite of all your efforts, you *do* make a mistake, it can be erased, but make sure the rubber or eraser is white and absolutely clean. If necessary, sharpen one end with a knife. This way it will reach deeper into the groove between the squares. When all the design has been transferred, simply remove the sewing thread and you are ready to start embroidering.

If you are using a dark-coloured canvas, ordinary pencil tracing will not show up. You must resort to a white pencil. As coloured pencils cannot be sharpened sufficiently for running from hole to hole to be effective, the best procedure is to dot the centre of each square that is to be embroidered. In this case you will need to apply strong pressure, as the marks tend to wear out.

The Baby's Room project shown on the previous spread is relatively simple: some of the blocks of ten by ten squares have very few stitches in them and the design uses only four colours, mostly in separate sections. So you can safely copy the whole chart and start embroidering. If your design is more complicated and likely to be confusing, you may choose to transfer only part of it, say one colour at a time. In the Motion Pillow project (see page 108), which has three oscillating lines of different colours, I first transferred and embroidered the red line. Then I did the yellow and finally the blue. The red line served as a guide when I came to chart the other colours.

THE STITCHES

Only three kinds of stitch were used in creating all the alphabets in this book: back stitch, cross stitch and Algerian eye.

To begin *back stitch* (see diagram A), bring your needle up from the wrong side of the fabric at 1, go down at 2, up at 3, down at 4, etc.

Each *cross stitch* corresponds to one square on a chart (see diagram B). The needle goes up at 1, down at 2, up at 3, down at 4 to form a cross, then up at 5 and so on to form the next one. When working a larger area in one colour, sew an entire row in *tent stitch* (half-cross stitch), crossing these stitches on your way back. Make sure that all your stitches are crossed in the same direction.

Algerian eye, which looks like a little star, covers four squares with each complete stitch (see diagram C). Bring up the needle in the centre of the 'star' and go down into any hole in the perimeter, then bring the needle up in the centre again. Continue in this way until you have worked round the eight holes on the perimeter. When the last stitch is completed, start another group of four squares.

A fourth stitch used in some projects in this book is *double running stitch*, which looks identical on both sides of the fabric. This very simple stitch is formed in two stages. First, embroider the design in *running stitch*, then turn and, on your way back, fill in the gaps with more running stitches.

THREADS AND NEEDLES

Any six-stranded cotton embroidery floss is suitable for our purpose, the best known brands being Anchor and DMC. The strands can easily be separated to suit the count of the canvas. For 14-count Aida a three-strand thickness gives the best coverage: it results in neat squares with little or no fabric showing through.

Metallic threads give your work a luxurious sheen, but are often too thin to cover the canvas properly and must be doubled or tripled. For a lesser-count Aida you may prefer Lurex knitting yarn. A helpful hint: before threading the needle, paint the free end of the metallic thread with colourless nail polish and let it dry. This will retard, if not altogether prevent, the fraying of the thread.

Use a blunt needle (tapestry needle) that fits comfortably in the holes of the canvas. Never use sharp-pointed needles as they will pierce both the threads of the canvas and any stitches you have already worked. This will slow down your pace and can result in distorted, uneven stitches.

WORKING IN THREADS

There are two ways of working in threads: the correct one and mine. To accommodate the purists and for the benefit of those who want everything 'just right', I will first describe the correct technique.

Cut about 40 cm (16 inches) of embroidery floss (longer threads tend to tangle) and flatten one end between your teeth to ease the threading of the needle. Roll the canvas away from you until you reach a comfortable hold for your first stitch. (Always roll the canvas upwards so that the wrong side is exposed. You can then hold it tightly without fear of dirtying it or smudging the pencilled lines.)

Pull the threaded needle through the canvas, leaving a length of about 2.5 cm (1 inch) on the wrong side. Begin working the stitches and, at the same time, hold the remaining thread in place until it is covered by several stitches. Cut away the excess thread and continue stitching. When you wish to finish the thread, weave it into the reverse of the stitches.

The virtuous are now kindly requested to skip this paragraph. For those who are interested in economy of time and thread, here is the unorthodox way of starting a new thread: with the needle catch two threads on the wrong side of the Aida cloth and sew two back stitches. Done.

PREVENTING TANGLING

To prevent tangling, as you stitch, hold a finger on the wrong side of the canvas near the point where the needle emerges. Feel the thread running against your finger. You will instantly detect any tangling or, worse, forming of a knot. Reverse your movement, bringing the needle back to the wrong side, and undo the knot.

After you have sewn a number of stitches the thread may become twisted. To remedy this, simply let the thread and needle dangle from your work, allowing the thread to untwist.

SPECIAL TECHNIQUES

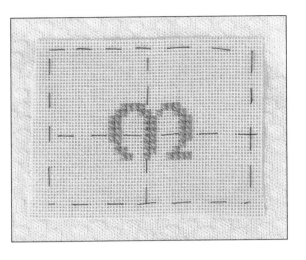

Wasted canvas: once you have finished your embroidery the canvas can be removed thread by thread, leaving the monogram on the fabric.

WASTED CANVAS

Even closely woven fabrics such as satin or velvet can be embroidered using the counted-thread technique with the help of wasted canvas. Many hobby shops sell a canvas especially made for this purpose. Simply tack/baste a piece of this canvas on to the fabric (it is wise to pre-shrink this) and embroider your design. When you have finished, remove the canvas thread by thread. Wetting it in warm water dissolves the starch and makes the process easier. To protect your nails, use tweezers for pulling at the threads.

Any knitted garment can be embroidered using Swiss darning. When planning your embroidery, consider the shape of the human body. On a flat surface, the monogram on the multi-coloured sweater may look too close to the centre, yet it will be in the right place when it is worn.

SWISS DARNING

This technique is used for embroidering knitted garments, whether hand- or machine-knitted. Swiss darning mimics the shape of stocking stitch so that the finished embroidery has the characteristic look of knitting. It is important to match the thickness of the embroidery thread or yarn with that of the background.

Secure the thread with two running stitches on the wrong side and bring the needle out at the bottom of the first stitch to be covered. Take the needle up to the top of the same stitch and pass it under the base of the stitch above. Then bring the needle down through the first point of entry to complete the stitch.

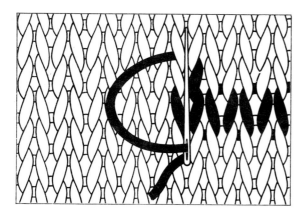

Swiss darning

FABRIC PAINTS

In recent years new technology has made painting on fabric easier than ever. Water-based textile paints and markers are available at art and hobby shops and their colour range grows steadily. Fabric paints can be combined with embroidery either to speed up work on larger surfaces (see the *Agnus Dei* project, page 49) or as an underlay for blackwork.

Marker pens do not penetrate the fabric as thoroughly as paint does, but are safer to use. Interesting effects can be achieved by overlaying strokes of different colours. In the illustration opposite, the marbled frame was made by circular strokes with a red marker and criss-cross strokes with a blue one, while the edges were protected with masking tape.

Marker pens are so easy to use that even children can create their own textile designs. Instead of charting a child's drawing as in Debbie Greenwood's pillow (opposite), let the child draw direct on to the canvas. Press with a hot iron to fix the ink in place, then add some lettering and an embroidered frame. The design may not be very well balanced nor, in all probability, will the drawing be the best the child can do, but there will nevertheless be a charming element of spontaneity.

Since marker ink stays on the surface, there is no need to take excessive precautions to avoid staining. When using paint, you should be more cautious. As it soaks through the fabric, wet patches of colour form underneath. It is therefore preferable to attach the canvas to a piece of disposable cardboard and, while painting, move the cardboard rather than the canvas. This will prevent smearing the paint underneath, some of which could show on the surface of the canvas and spoil your work.

A flat, soft brush is best for larger surfaces. For small ones an inexpensive eye-shadow applicator is quite satisfactory. It is important to experiment on small scraps of canvas until you are familiar with both the paint and the tools. When the paint is dry, iron it to fix it permanently on to the fabric. Some paints can be washed immediately, others need a curing time. Follow the manufacturer's instructions to the letter.

OPPOSITE, TOP LEFT *Washable fabric paints and marker pens can be combined with embroidery for a new and interesting look.*

TOP RIGHT *No more rummaging through the luggage for clean underwear. These are two easy-to-sew and easy-to-find travel cases for small personal items. Fabric markers cover a large area quickly, and the embroidery on these projects is minimal. Design your own monogram by intertwining two letters.*

RIGHT *Make a child proud of his or her artistic talent by embroidering a drawing and turning it into a cherished keepsake. Ryba and Britten alphabets were used for this project (see pages 67 and 69).*

THE TECHNIQUE OF BLACKWORK

Embroidering a blackwork pattern entails running the embroidery floss from one hole to another over a counted number of threads or, in the case of Aida cloth, over a counted number of units.

The stitches used are few and easy to master. In addition to cross stitch and back stitch, used in all the projects in this book, blackwork patterns are also formed by running stitch and its derivative, double running stitch. The latter, also called Holbein stitch, was named after Hans Holbein, the court painter under the reign of Henry VIII. Holbein's sitters were often dressed in garments decorated with blackwork embroidery.

As double running stitch looks identical on both sides of the fabric it is especially helpful when the wrong side of the pattern is to be exposed to view as in

ruffs, cuffs or collars. In projects intended for framing, where the wrong side is of little concern, you can safely combine double running stitch with back stitch, as both look the same on the surface. (For a detailed description of the stitches see page 93.)

BELOW AND OPPOSITE *Pattern darning: beginners will be greatly encouraged to know that these pretty patterns are produced with nothing more complex than different combinations of running stitch.*

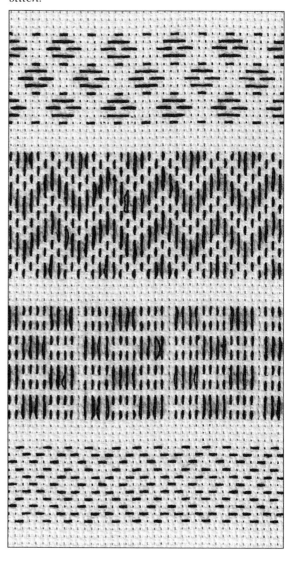

BELOW *Blackwork uses simple stitching to achieve quite complicated effects.*

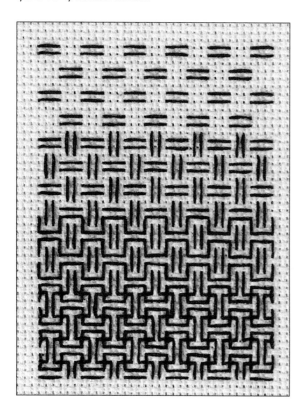

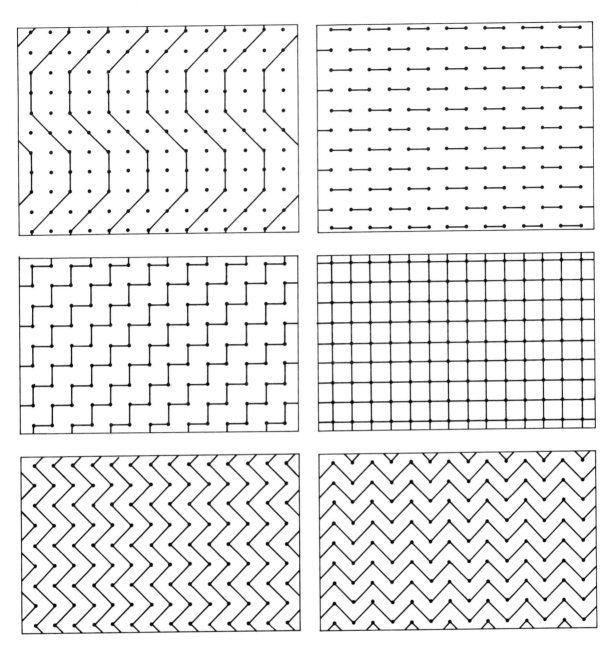

PATTERN DARNING

At this point mention should be made of yet another type of counted-thread embroidery, pattern darning. In this technique patterns are formed with running stitches of various lengths, as seen in the sampler opposite. Because of its great simplicity, pattern darning is recommended for beginners: it is very encouraging to be able to make decorative patterns so easily.

DUPLICATING BLACKWORK PATTERNS

Some blackwork patterns are so simple that they need no explanation. Others look alarmingly complex. It is important to realize that even the most complicated pattern is formed by simple elements. The trick is to isolate these and then to analyze the number, length and direction of the stitches. Once we understand how a pattern was built we can reproduce it easily.

The complex two-directional pattern shown here was embroidered in four stages. First, there are double rows of running stitches worked horizontally over three holes. The second stage repeats the same stitches vertically. In the third stage the thread is run vertically, connecting the lower horizontal stitch in one row with the upper horizontal stitch in the row below. Finally, the thread is run horizontally, connecting the second vertical stitch with the first vertical stitch of the row below.

From simple to complex, each stage becomes a new pattern. Notice how the patterns progress from light to dark as the density of the stitches increases.

BLACKWORK PATTERNS

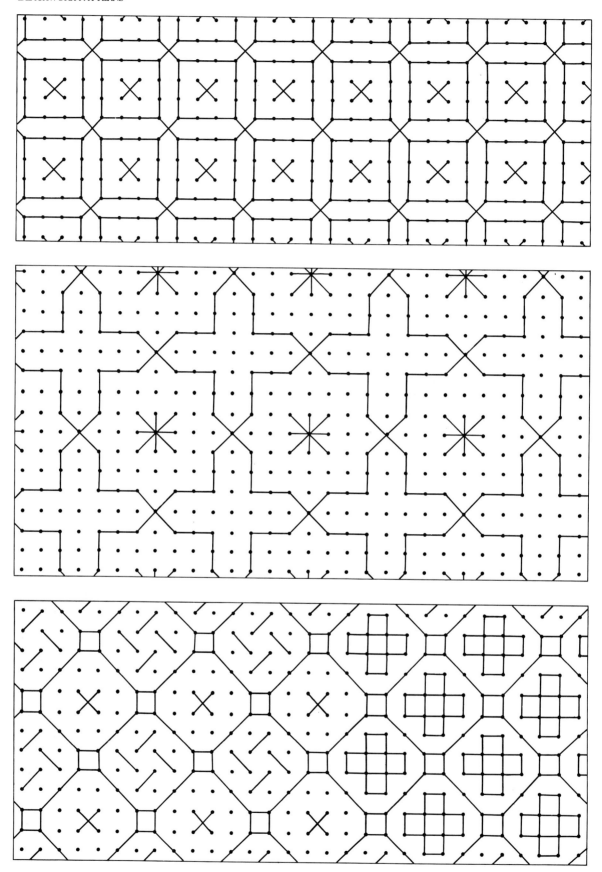

BLACKWORK PATTERNS

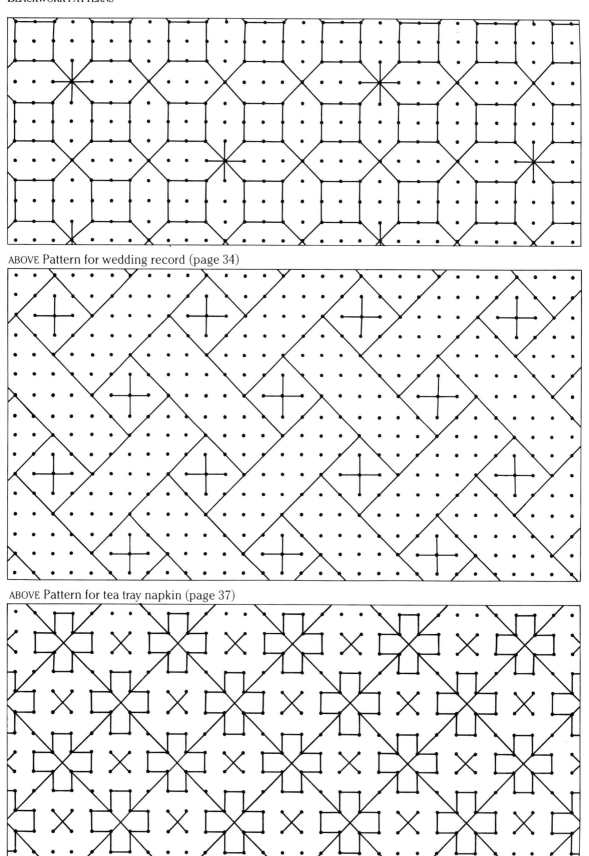

ABOVE Pattern for wedding record (page 34)

ABOVE Pattern for tea tray napkin (page 37)

ABOVE Pattern for diary (page 108)

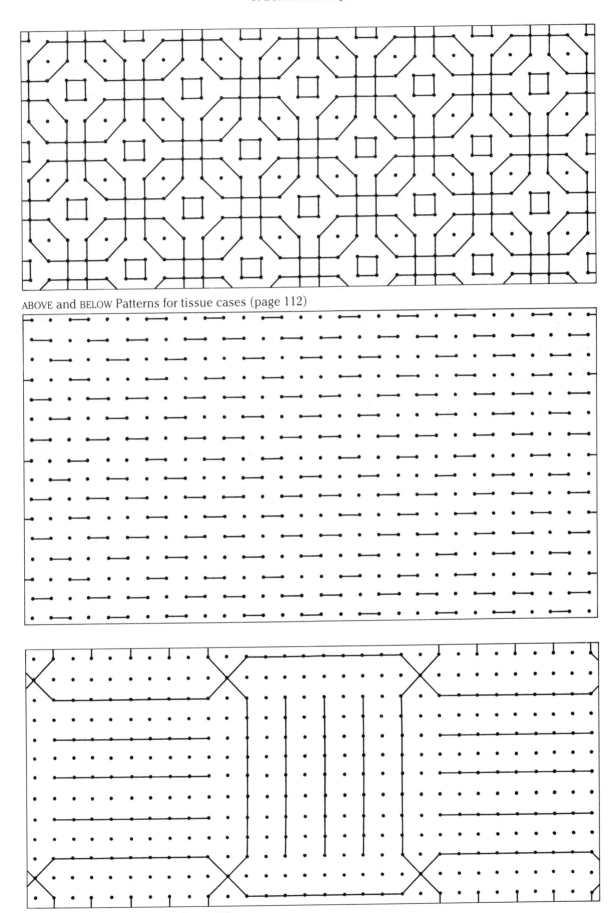

ABOVE and BELOW Patterns for tissue cases (page 112)

ABOVE Pattern for travel case (page 97)

Most needlecraft shops sell an assortment of items with Aida-weave insets. Towels, bookmarks, little boxes, spectacle cases, aprons, bibs and other objects can be personalized with counted-thread alphabets.

	374
	437
	958
	312

The 'window' for a greeting card can be a straightforward rectangle. On the other hand, it can play an active part in the design, as in the Happy Hanukah card. Experiment with other simple shapes such as circles, hexagons, ovals, hearts or scallops. See page 106 for instructions on making a card.

MONOGRAMS

In earlier times household linens were a valuable possession, intended to last a lifetime. Wealthy families employed the services of a laundress who collected dirty linen and returned it washed, starched and ironed. For the purpose of identification each piece had to be marked with the owner's name or initials.

Practical as their origins were, monograms soon evolved into little pieces of art. To the elaborate and often intertwined letters were added flowers, coronets, frames and, where applicable, coats of arms. Embroidering a bride's trousseau, which consisted of at least a dozen of each item, was a major enterprise to be started in a girl's early teens if she wanted to be ready for her wedding day.

Our fast-paced life does not allow for such treatment of household linen, nor are today's brides expected to possess dozens of embroidered sheets or petticoats. Monograms are restricted to luxury items. They no longer hide in bedrooms or under clothes. On the contrary, we see them displayed on jackets, shirts, sweaters, scarfs or purses. Whether embroidered, engraved or painted, monograms turn ordinary objects into unique ones. They proclaim ownership and seem to say, 'See, I or someone who loves and appreciates me, took the pain of personalizing this thing for me.' In short, monograms are not for the bashful.

It is in monogramming that the technique of wasted canvas (see page 95) comes in handy. Any kind of fabric can be embroidered this way and people are often amazed at the precise shapes of the letters. Don't give your secret away!

GREETING CARDS

Greeting cards have become an integral part of our social life. More and more, we rely upon these little devices to convey our sentiments and wishes. A prettily wrapped hand-made card is a gift in itself. Whenever you can, include the name or, at least, the initials of the person your card is intended for. People love to receive personalized items. What better way to say you care?

The craft paper that will frame the card should harmonize with the embroidery. Unfortunately, the colour range of these papers is somewhat limited and it is certainly easier to match the embroidery floss with the paper than the other way around. In short, choose the paper first.

Sources of inspiration are limitless and easily available. A greeting-card rack in your local stationer's will provide you with dozens of ideas.

The cards presented here were designed with speed in mind. They were executed on 14-count Aida and each was completed within a few days. If time is not a problem, design your card for the 18- or 22-count grid. You will be able to use larger and more elaborate alphabets without making your project too big.

When the embroidery is finished, decide how large the frame should be. Cut the craft paper into a rectangle twice the size and fold it along the central axis. Cut a window for the embroidery. Centre the canvas on the window, face down, and attach it with masking tape. Run a glue stick around the edges and press both halves together. Place the finished card on a flat surface and weigh it down until the glue dries.

BOOK COVER

These make an ideal gift for avid readers. The formula below can be adapted to any size: simply substitute the height of the book for 'X', the width for 'Y' and the width of the spine for 'Z'.

Cover: X + 1 cm (½ in) × Y + Y + Z + 1.5 cm (¾ in)
Flap: X + 1 cm (½ in) × ½Y

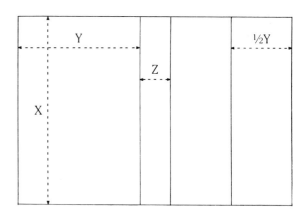

Making a book cover

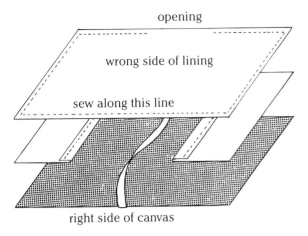

opening

wrong side of lining

sew along this line

right side of canvas

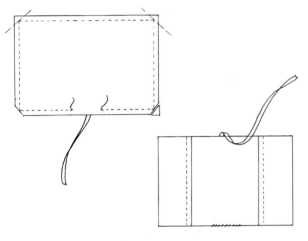

Sewing the book cover

A typical paperback measures about 18 by 10 cm (7 by 4 in) with a 2.5 cm (1 in) spine. Using the formula enables you to calculate that you will need a rectangle of canvas 24 by 19 cm (10 + 10 + 2.5 + 1.5 by 18 + 1) or 9¾ by 7½ in (4 + 4 + 1 + ¾ by 7 + ½). To this rectangle must be added a seam allowance of 1.5 cm (¾ in) on all sides. Thus the final size of the canvas will be 27 by 22 cm (24 + 1.5 + 1.5 by 19 + 1.5 + 1.5) or 11¼ by 9 in (9¾ + ¾ + ¾ by 7½ + ¾ + ¾).

Embroider the canvas, following one of the ideas shown on page 112 or making up your own. After you have finished, cut the canvas to the required size. Then cut another rectangle the same size as the canvas, and two flaps using a lining material of your choice.

Fold one flap over 1.5 cm (¾ in) along the longer side. Pin and tack/baste. Sew along the hem with a zigzag stitch. Repeat with the second flap. Remove the tacking/basting stitches and iron.

Place a narrow ribbon about 27 cm (11 in) long in the upper centre of the canvas. Sandwich all the pieces together as shown in diagram A. Pin and tack/baste. Remember that the seam allowance is 1.5 cm (¾ in), so sew that distance from the edge. Start sewing about

4 cm (1½ in) from the lower centre of the cover. Sew along all sides and stop 4 cm (1½ in) from the lower centre, leaving an opening of 8 cm (3 in). Cut off the corners close to the sewing line and turn the cover inside out, as in diagram B.

Tack/baste the cover along the sewing line and iron it. Sew up the opening at the base. Remove the tacking/basting stitches and your book cover is ready.

A word of caution before you start working on a book cover. The formula given here makes for a perfectly fitted cover only if the embroidery is kept to a minimum. The more you embroider a canvas, the more it 'shrinks' in size. For such techniques as darning and blackwork, where the thread is woven into the canvas and the embroidery covers the whole area, shrinkage can be a very important factor. Since books, photo albums and diaries come in many sizes and the various blackwork patterns create different bulk on both sides of the canvas, there is no telling how much shrinkage one should expect. In the case of the wedding photo album cover (see page 55) about 1.5 cm (¾ in) had to be added on all sides. In any case, check and recheck the size. Once you have cut the corners close to the sewing line, there is no going back. Also, the thicker the embroidery floss and the bulkier the lining fabric, the more caution you should exercise. Note: to prevent the ribbon from fraying, tie a small knot near the free end or paint the end with colourless nail polish.

PILLOWCASE

Since some pillows are more fully stuffed than others, measure the girth of your pillow both vertically and horizontally before you start to calculate how much fabric you will need. Divide each measurement by two to obtain the size of the square or rectangle that will form the front of the pillowcase. Let's say that the girth of a 38 cm (15 in) square pillow is 80 cm (32 in). Divide this by two, and you will find that the pillowcase will have to be 40 cm (16 in) square. Add a seam allowance of 1.5 cm (¾ in) on each side, and the front of the pillowcase, including seam allowances, will measure 43 cm (40 + 1.5 + 1.5) or 17½ in (16 + ¾ + ¾) square. Let us call this measurement A.

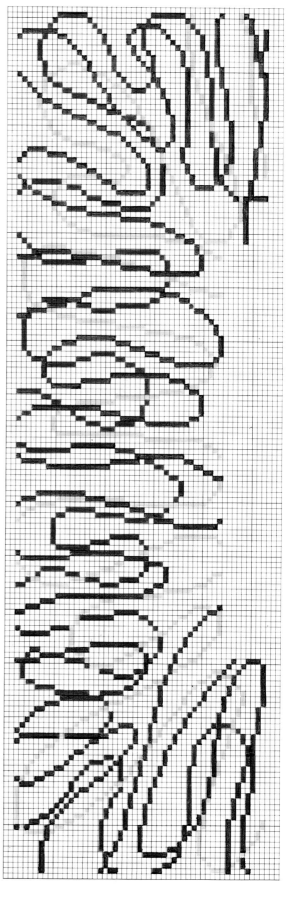

ABOVE *The diary is another variation on the blackwork theme: embroidered on a six-count Aida cloth it makes a large and bold pattern.*

BELOW *Primary colours and a vibrating frame are the main features of this contemporary design. The lettering, with no spacing between the lines, forms a unified block, a square within a square.*

 321

 742

797

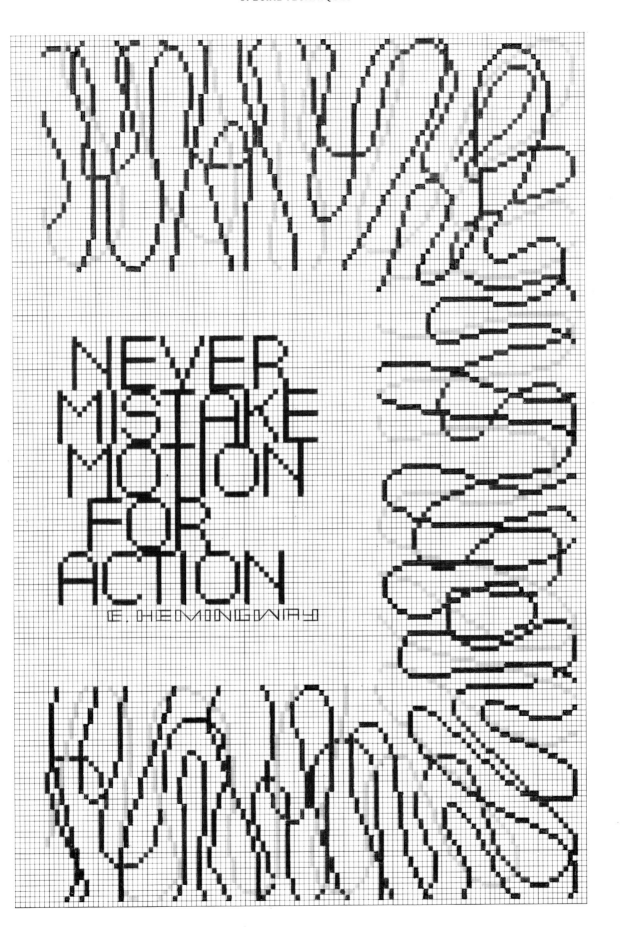

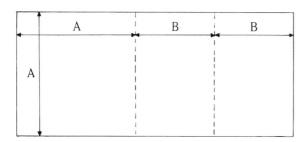

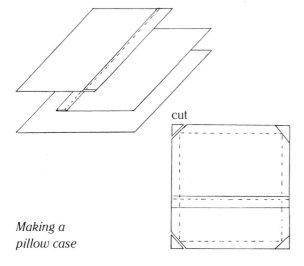

*Making a
pillow case*

The back is formed by two panels which overlap each other by 12.5 cm (5 in). We know that the vertical measurement for each panel is 43 cm (17½ in). To calculate the width, divide A in half and add 12.5 cm (5 in) for the overlap plus 2.5 cm (1 in) for the fold in the opening. This gives 21.5 cm (8¾ in) – ½A – plus 12.5 cm + 2.5 cm (5 in + 1 in), that is 36.5 cm (14¾ in). This is measurement B. The fabric you need to make this particular pillowcase is therefore a rectangle that measures A by A + B + B – the height of the pillow by the width plus the width of the two flaps – or 43 by 116 cm (17½ by 47 in).

If you embroider the front panel on Aida cloth, you may like to use a different fabric for the back. In this case, your Aida cloth will be a square measuring A by A, and your back panels will be a rectangle of A by B + B (43 by 36.5 + 36.5 cm or 17½ by 14¾ + 14¾ in), which you should cut in half.

To assemble the pillowcase, work on the back panels first. Fold the sides that will face the opening over 2.5 cm (1 in) on the wrong side, pin and tack/baste. Machine stitch 1.5 cm (¾ in) from the fold, remove the tacking/basting stitches and iron.

Place the front panel right side up and cover it with the back panels, wrong side up. Align the corners of front and back neatly. This will make the two back panels overlap. Pin and tack/baste. Machine stitch along all sides. Cut the corners close to the sewing line

and turn the case inside out. Tack/baste along the sewing line and iron. Remove the tacking/basting stitches.

TRAVEL CASE

Cut a rectangle of Aida cloth 24 × 18 cm (9½ × 7 in) for the smaller case, and 51 × 28 cm (20 × 11 in) for the larger. Zigzag along the edges and work the embroidery. Fold the sides that face the opening 2.5 cm (1 in) over on the wrong side. Keep them in place by oversewing along both sides. Overlap ends as shown in the diagram, pin and tack/baste. Machine stitch 1.5 cm (¾ in) from each side. Cut the corners near the stitching line and turn the case inside out. Tack/baste along the sewing line and iron. Remove the tacking/basting stitches.

TISSUE CASE

Cut a rectangle of Aida cloth 24 × 18 cm (9½ × 7 in). Zigzag along the edges and work the embroidery. When finished, fold the canvas in half, wrong side up, and tack/baste pieces together 2.5 cm (1 in) from the outer side. Machine stitch 4 cm (1½ in) from each side. Iron the seam open and remove the tacking/basting stitches. Oversew the hems. Centre the opening, pin and tack/baste. Machine stitch along both sides 1.5 cm (¾ in) from the edge. Remove the tacking/basting stitches and cut the corners close to

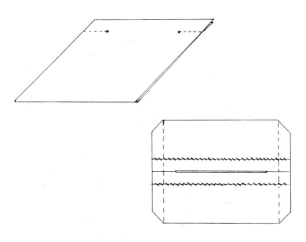

Making a tissue case

110

the stitching line. Turn the case inside out. Tack/baste along the stitching line and iron. Remove the tacking/basting stitches.

WALL-HANGING

Cut out the panel as shown in the diagram. Fold the sides inwards, pin and tack/baste. Oversew the hems and remove the tacking/basting stitches. Rinse in warm water, allow to dry, then iron. Remove the weft threads from the fringe area.

Attach the cord to the wooden rod with masking tape. Slide the rod inside the opening at the top and gather the fabric to expose the other end of the rod.

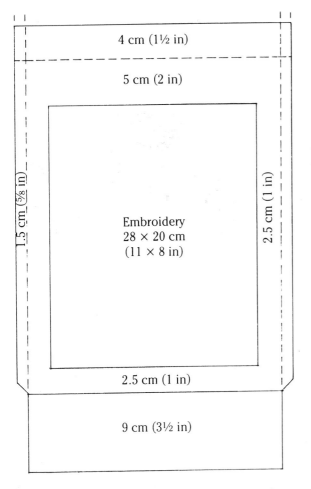

Making a wall-hanging

Attach the other end of the rope to the rod and smooth the fabric over it.

If you want to wash the wall-hanging, simply remove the masking tape and free the rod.

FABRIC-COVERED FRAME

Cut two identical rectangles of heavy cardboard and cut a window for the embroidery in one of them. Join the two rectangles with masking tape to make your frame. Measure the frame and add 2.5 cm (1 in) on every side. Cut a piece of fabric according to this measurement and place it on a flat surface, wrong side up. Centre the cardboard over the fabric and cut off the corners of the fabric close to the cardboard. Fold the fabric over and secure it with masking tape. Cut a smaller rectangle for the window and clip the corners. Fold the fabric inside and attach it with the tape.

Making a fabric-covered frame

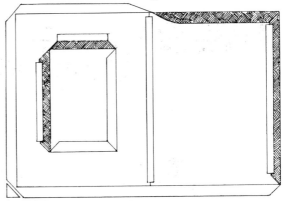

Centre the embroidery over the window, wrong side up, and attach it with masking tape. Then fold the frame and glue both sides together. Weight down the finished frame with a flat, heavy object like a book until the glue dries.

SIGN

Cut two identical rectangles in a medium-weight cardboard. Fold the embroidered canvas around one of the rectangles and attach it with masking tape. Glue the second rectangle on top of the folded canvas. Attach a peel-and-stick picture mount at each corner.

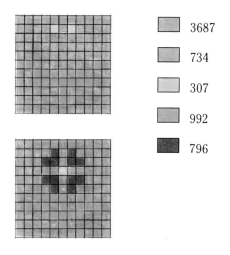

▢	3687
▢	734
▢	307
▢	992
▢	796

RIGHT *The basic pattern for a book cover can be adapted to any number of purposes. The giant monogram is built up of a number of flowery squares – simple letters such as E, F, H, I, L or T work best. If you wish, you can add other letters chosen from a smaller alphabet.*

The black cover is worked in variegated embroidery floss, which creates interesting effects by playing with different intensities of a single colour from dark to light. Apart from a tiny gold embellishment in the bottom right-hand corner, this is all embroidered in one colour, but is far from dull.

BELOW *Small and useful, these two tissue cases demonstrate how blackwork and pattern darning can come alive if you introduce colour.*

The main purpose of embroidery is to embellish the useful. Embroidered signs, however, are useful objects in their own right. They should obviously be easy to read, and the clear but not too plain Gershwin was a good choice here (see page 131 for chart).

BELOW A miniature sampler is a perfect gift for Mother's Day. If you plan to use a fabric-covered frame, choose your fabric first, then select embroidery floss to match. See page 111 for instructions on making a frame.

Do you need a personalized gift for tomorrow? Buy an Aida-weave bookmark and add a monogram. This initial is chosen from the Bizet alphabet (see page 121 for chart). A good project for beginners.

TCHAIKOVSKY

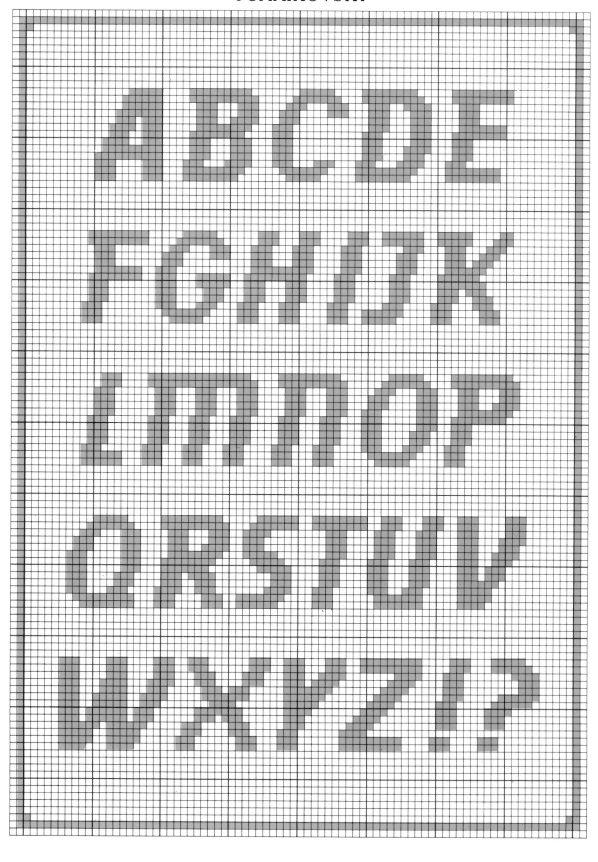

GRIEG

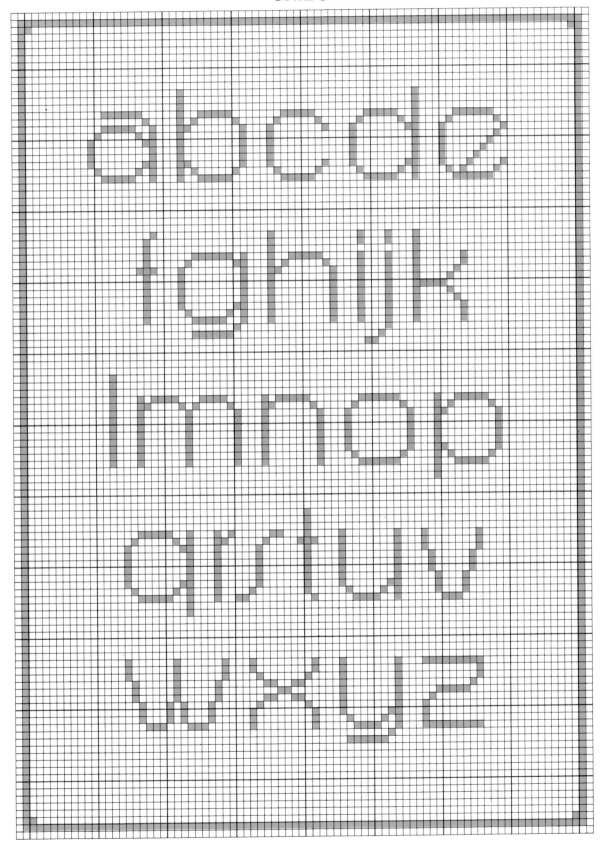

WAGNER

WAGNER

BERLIN

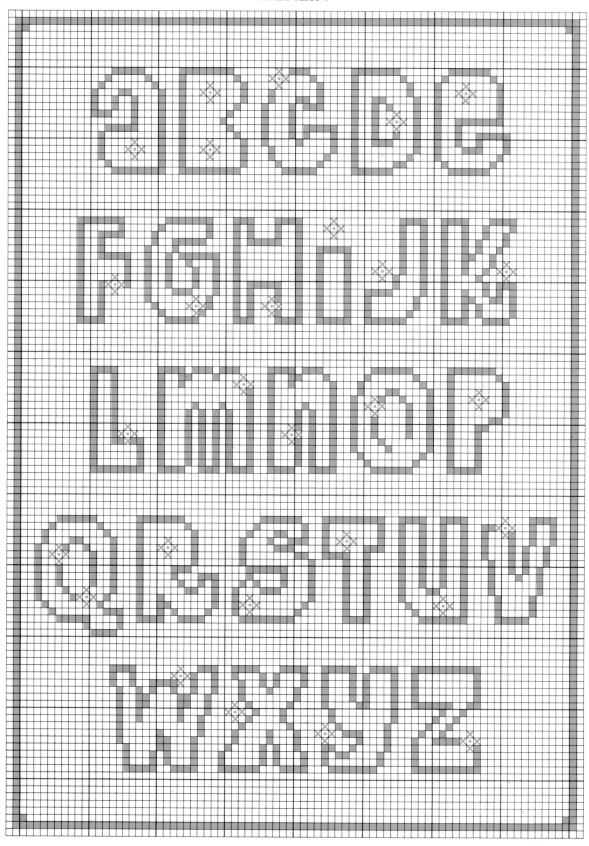

PURCELL

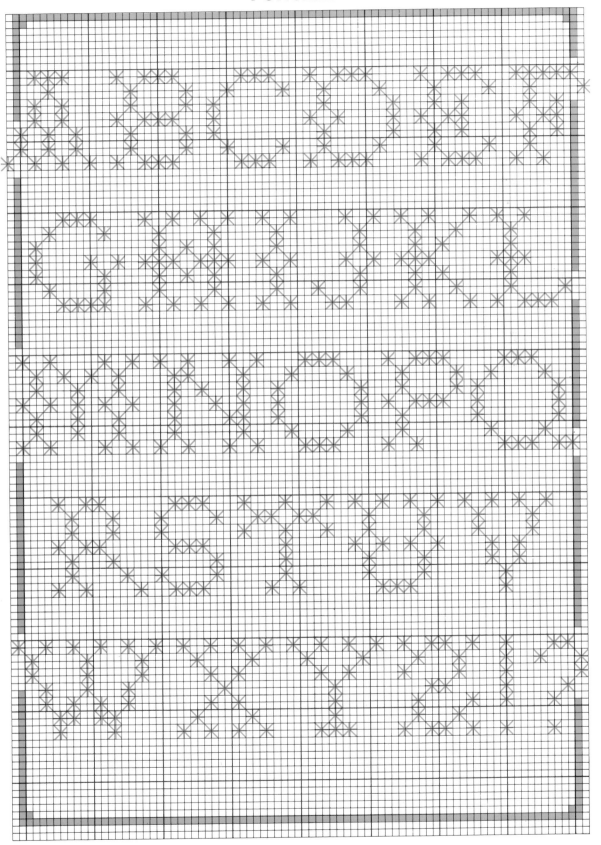

SIBELIUS

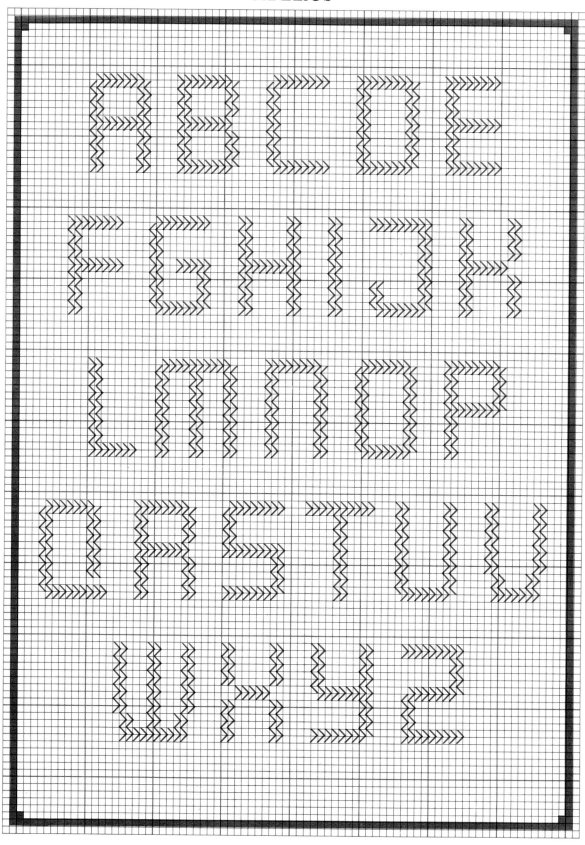

BIZET

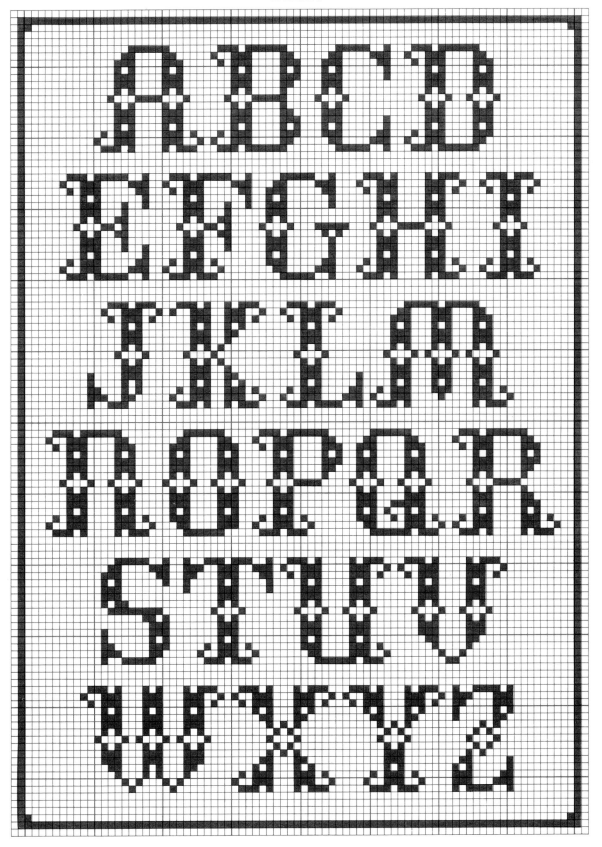

BACH

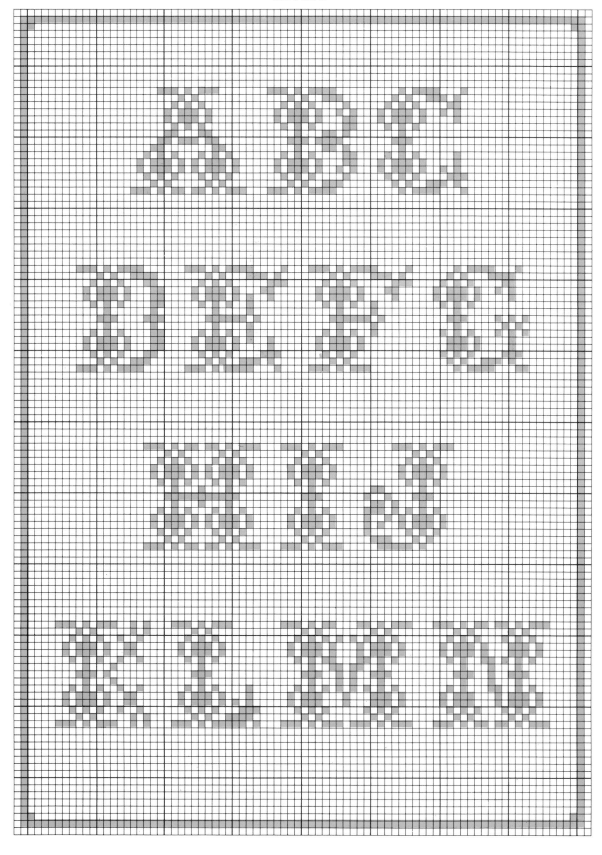

BACH

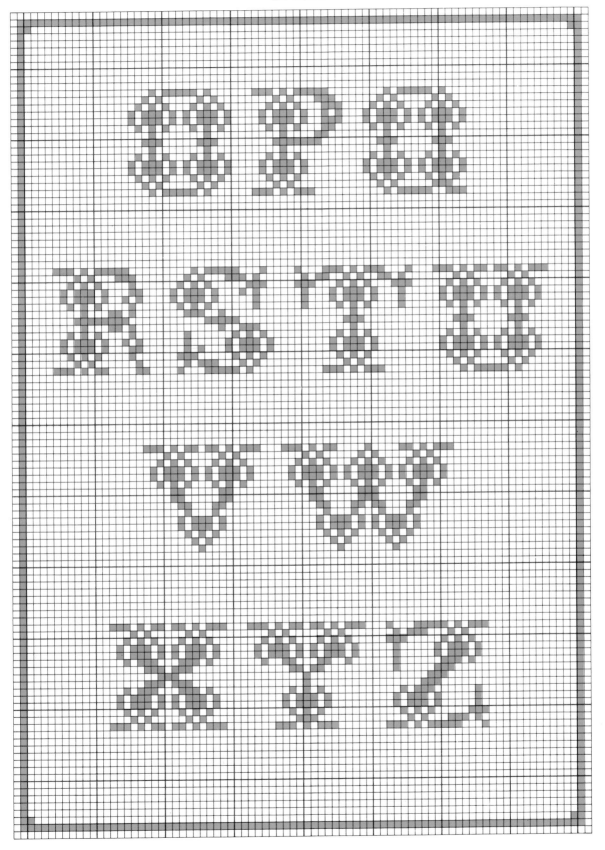

MOZART

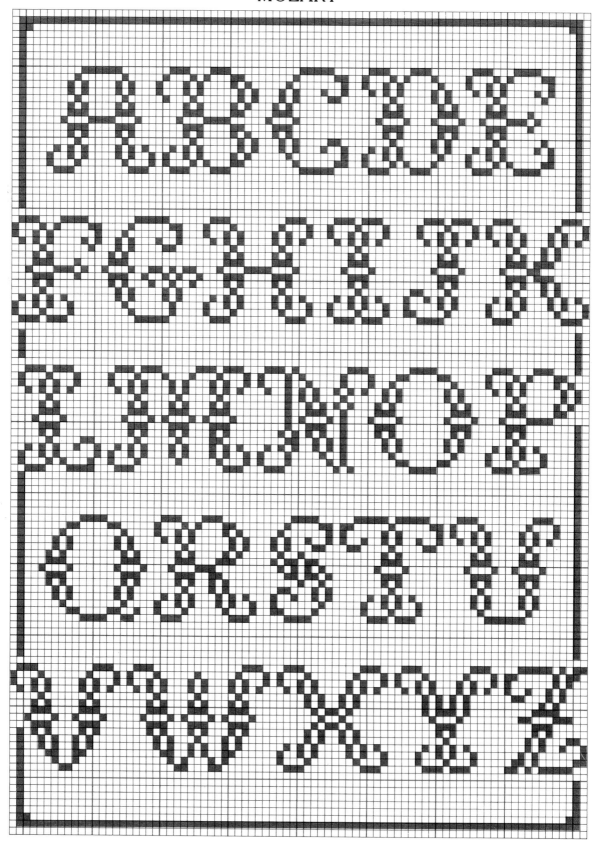

RIMSKY-KORSAKOV

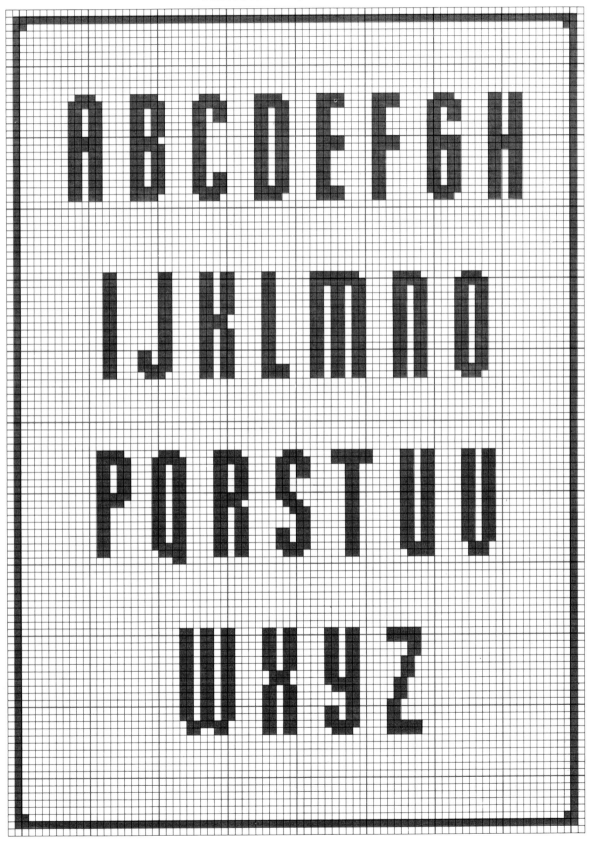

VERDI

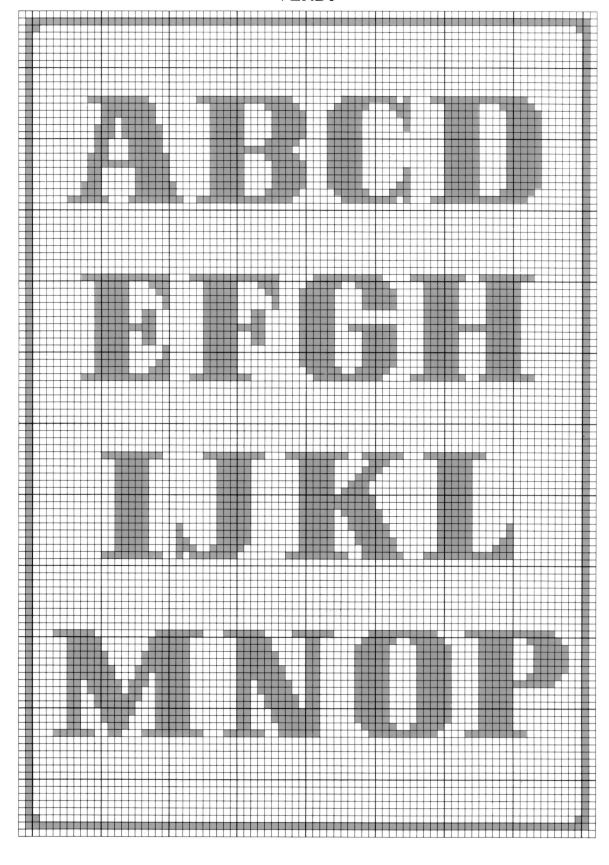

VERDI

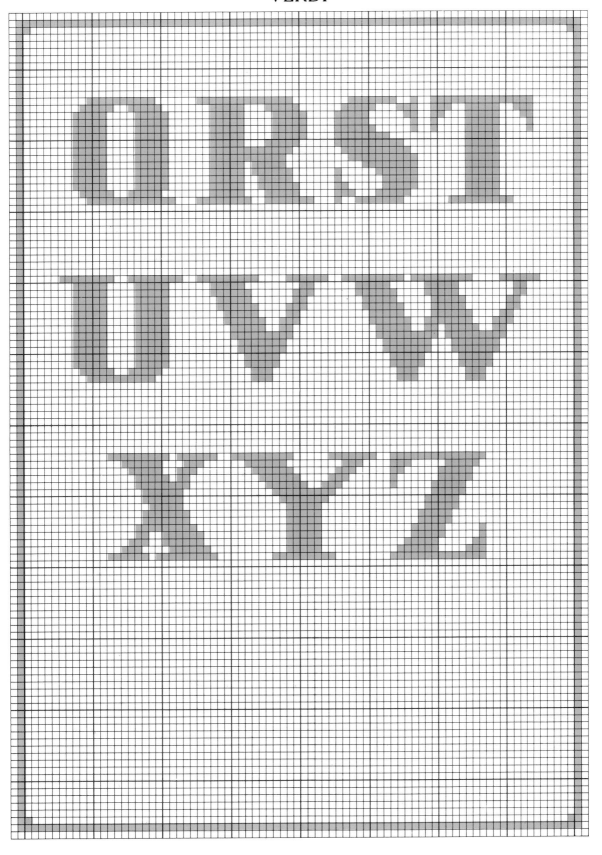

CHOPIN

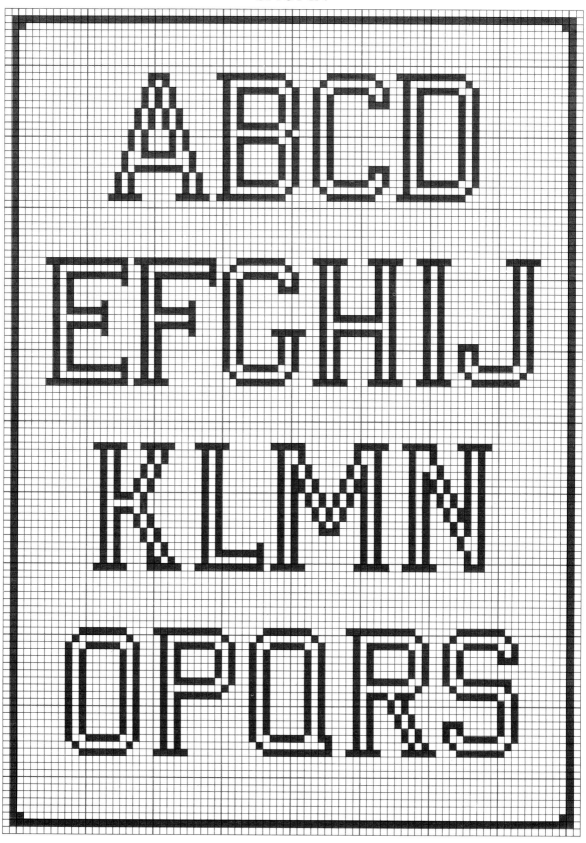

CHOPIN

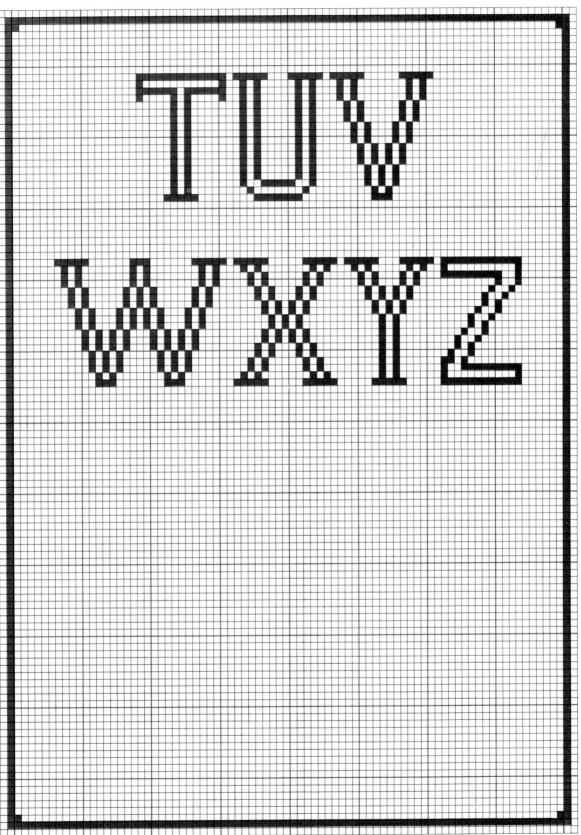

CHOPIN

GERSHWIN

COMPOSERS

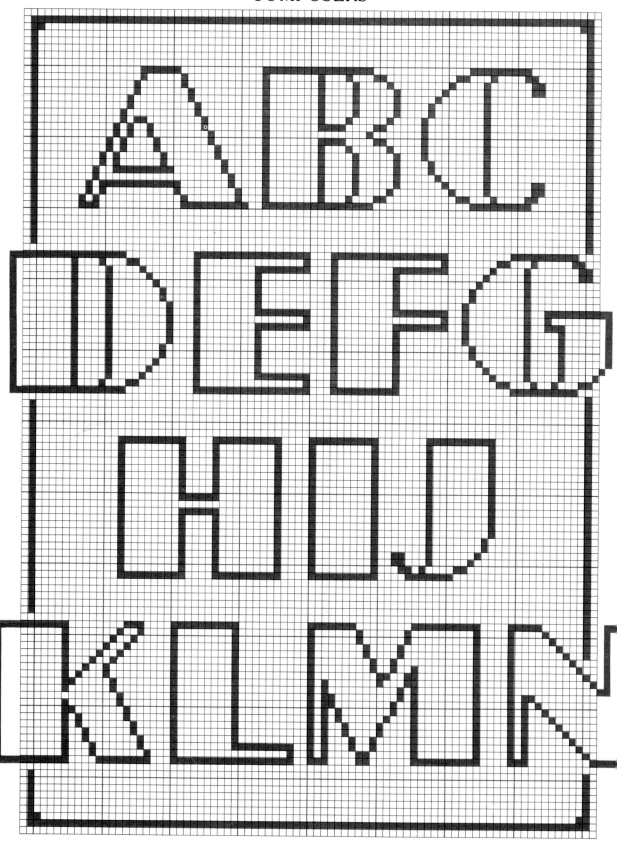

COMPOSERS

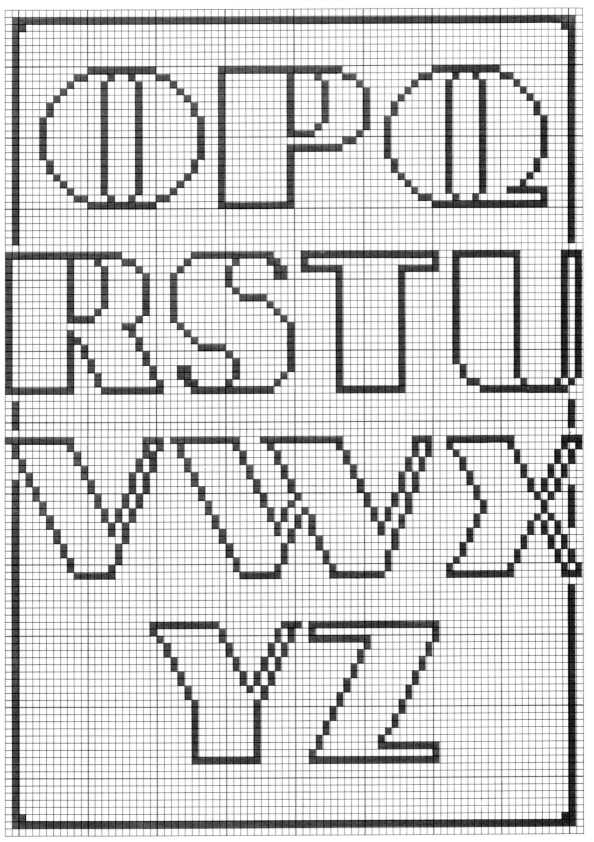

RAVEL

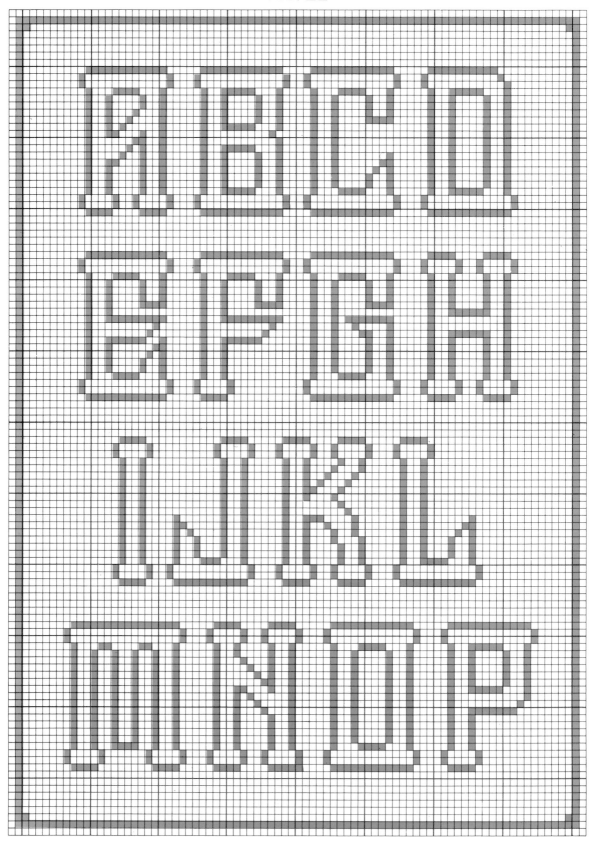

RAVEL

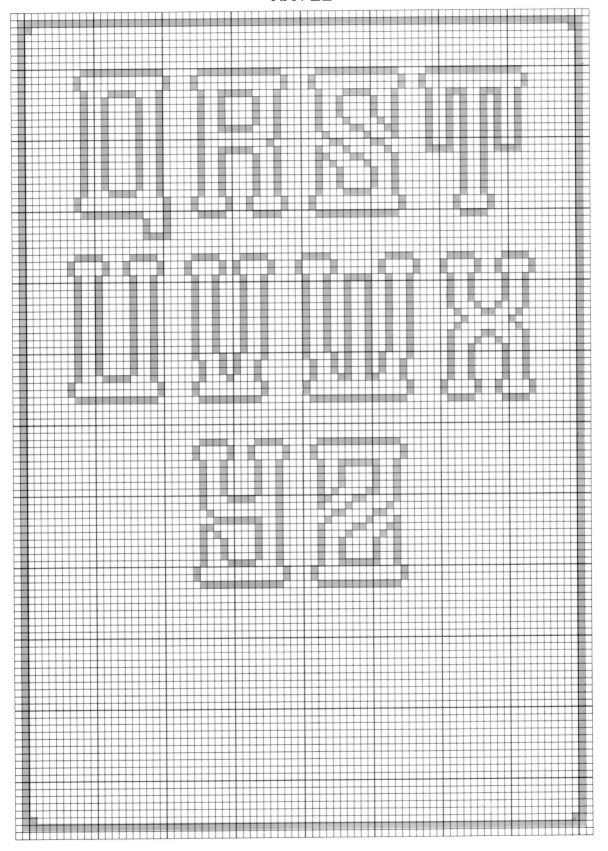

VIVALDI

VIVALDI

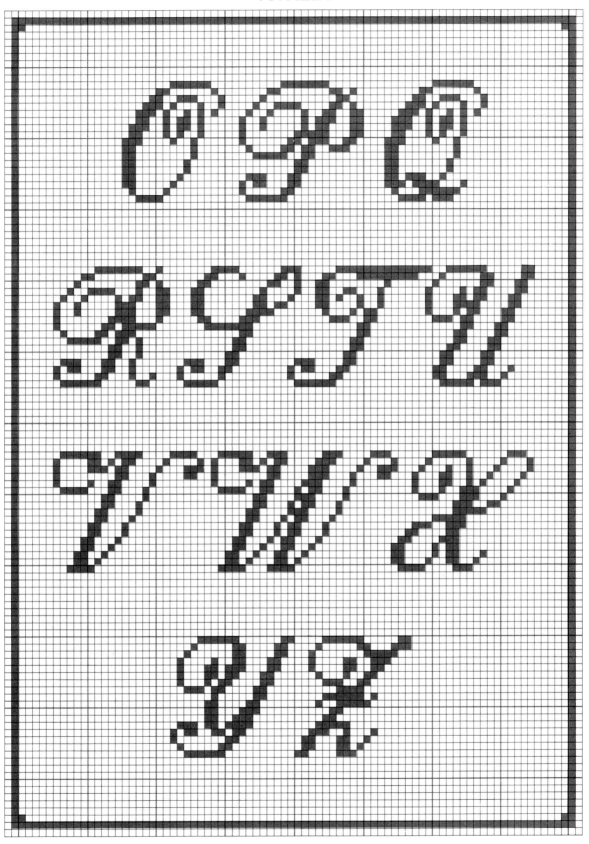

VIVALDI

TECHNICAL INFORMATION

The following details should enable you to work the projects charted in this book exactly as I have done. The numbers refer to DMC embroidery floss, but Anchor is equally suitable and you can, of course, vary the colours in any way you like. Unless otherwise stated, use three strands of embroidery floss and work in cross stitch.

COTTAGE SAMPLER (page 30)
Design area: 169 × 139 squares
Canvas required: Aida 14-count, white, 46 × 41 cm (18 × 16 in)
Thread required (skeins):
501 Blue Green Dark – 1
502 Blue Green – 1 (use two strands for blackwork in the trees)
522 Fern Green – 1 (use two strands for blackwork in the trees)
422 Tan Very Light – 1
435 Topaz Very Ultra Dark – 1 (use two strands for back stitch in the door)
783 Topaz – 1
347 Salmon Dark – 1 (use two strands for back stitch in the roof)
350 Salmon Medium Dark – 1
352 Peach Flesh – 1
353 Peach Flesh Light – 1
415 Silver – 1
3787 Brown Grey – 1

NO SMOKING SIGN (page 40)
See instructions for making a sign on page 111
Design area: 135 × 82 squares
Canvas required: Aida 14-count, white, 33 × 25 cm (13 × 10 in)
Thread required (skeins):
321 Christmas Red – 2
909 Christmas Green – 1
318 Steel Grey Light – 1
317 Pewter Grey – 1
310 Black – 1 (work the frame in tent stitch)

HAVE YOU HAD A KINDNESS SHOWN? SAMPLER (page 45)
Design area: 126 × 89 squares
Canvas required: Aida 14-count, white, 33 × 25 cm (13 × 10 in)
Thread required (skeins):
209 Lavender Medium Light – 2

915 Plum Dark – 2
964 Aquamarine Light – 3
413 Pewter Grey Dark – 1
310 Black – 1 (use two strands for back stitch for the lettering and the heads)

WEDDING PHOTO ALBUM COVER (page 54)
See instructions for making a book cover on page 106
Design area: variable, depending on the size of the album and the personal details to be included. Estimate the size of canvas and lining required following the formula on page 106. If necessary, adjust the dimensions of the inner frame by adding or removing one or more repeats (see Frames page 47).

Canvas required: Aida 18-count, white
Other materials required: black lining material (white or light-coloured lining would allow floats of black thread at the back of the embroidery to show through); small gold glass beads, no larger than one square unit on the canvas; beading needle, black and yellow sewing thread. If beads are not available, use metallic gold thread instead.
Thread required (skeins):
718 Plum – 1
3608 Plum Very Light – 1
333 Blue Violet – 1
502 Blue Green – 1
310 Black (approx) – 5 (use two strands)
Metallic gold thread (optional) – 1
Work the cross stitch areas first, then the darning pattern; sew on the beads last. Double the yellow sewing thread and anchor it with two back stitches. Sew on the bead and finish with two more back stitches. Do the same for each bead.

BIRTH RECORD SAMPLER (page 60)
Design area: variable, depending on the personal details to be included. Both frames are adjustable.
Canvas required: Aida 14-count, pink or blue. Measure the finished design and add 7.5 cm (3 in) tolerance on all sides.
Thread required (skeins, approximate):
Snow White – 2
3688 Mauve Medium – 2
933 Avocado Green – 1

HAPPY BIRTHDAY GRANDMOTHER CARD (page 104)
See instructions for making a greeting card on page
   106
Design area: 58 × 50 squares
Canvas required: Aida 14-count, white,
   16.5 × 14 cm (6½ × 5½ in)

Card window: 14 × 11.5 cm (5½ × 4½ in)
Craft paper: 38 × 25 cm (15 × 9¾ in)
Thread required (skeins):
312 Navy Blue Light – 1 (use two strands for antennae)
374 Mustard Dark – 1
437 Tan Brown Light – 1
958 Aquamarine Dark – 1

MOTION PILLOW (pages 108–109)
See instructions for making a pillowcase on page
   107
Design area: 160 × 160 squares
Canvas required: Aida 14-count, white, 42 × 42 cm
   (16½ × 16½ in)
Other materials required: white Aida cloth or
   matching fabric of your choice for the back panel
   (approximately 63 × 38 cm or 25 × 15 in); a 35
   cm (14 in) square pillow or cushion.
Thread required (skeins):
797 Blue Medium – 4 (use two strands for back
   stitch for the lettering)
742 Tangerine Light – 3
321 Christmas Red – 2

MONOGRAMMED BOOK COVER (page 114)
See instructions for making a book cover on page
   106
Design area: variable
Canvas required: Aida 14-count, écru, 31 × 23 cm
   (12 × 9 in)
Other materials required: lining material of your
   choice (approximately 43 × 20 cm or 17 × 8 in);
   blue ribbon (35 cm or 14 in)
Compose a monogram of your choice by alternating
   the two designs which make up the large letter.
Thread required (skeins):
307 Canary Bright – 1
3687 Mauve – 1
796 Royal Blue Dark – 1
992 Aquamarine Dark – 1
734 Olive Green Light – 2

CHILD'S DRAWING PILLOWCASE (page 97)
This project involves designing your own chart
See instructions for making a pillowcase on page
   107
Canvas required: Aida 14-count, écru
Other materials required: matching fabric for the
   back panel; a pillow or cushion; graph/grid paper,
   a pencil and coloured marker pens
Let the child draw directly on to the graph/grid paper
   with marker pens; alternatively, select one of his/
   her drawings and cover it with a transparent grid.
   For more instructions on charting a design, see
   Motifs (page 50). Add lettering using the Ryba and
   Britten alphabets (see pages 67 and 69) and a
   frame. Choose embroidery thread to match the
   colours used in the drawing.

ACKNOWLEDGEMENTS

The author and publishers would like to thank Elsie Svennas for permission to use three alphabets which are her copyright © 1973: these are the alphabets called Schubert, Mozart and Composers, which appear on pages 89, 124 and 132–133 respectively.

The publishers would also like to thank Lady Cooksey for allowing them to use her lovely home for photography.

Hearts and flowers would have kidnapped the humour of the Ask God sign and reduced it to sweet silliness. A not-too-cute mischievous cherub was a far better option. The combination of the tiny Ryba and chunky Gounod alphabets is chosen to complement the message (see pages 67 and 88 for charts).

BIBLIOGRAPHY

BAKER, ARTHUR *Arthur Baker's copybook of Renaissance calligraphy*, Dover Publications, New York, 1981

BAKER, ARTHUR, *Celtic hand, stroke by stroke*, Dover Publications, New York, 1980

BRITTAIN, JUDY, *Needle Craft*, Ebury Press, London, 1979

CHILD, HEATHER, *Calligraphy today: twentieth century tradition and practice*, A. & C. Black, London, 1988

Collective of authors, *Le Petit Robert: Dictionnaire universel des noms propres*, SEPRET, Paris, 1974

Collective of authors, *Praktická hospodynka*, F. Strnadel, Prague, 1929

DAVIS, FRANK and others, *Antiques*, Octopus Books, London, 1974

DROGIN, MARK, *Medieval calligraphy: its history and technique*, Allanheld and Schram, 1980

FAWDREY, MARGARET, *The book of samplers,* St Martin's Press, New York, 1980

FORSTNER, REGINA, *Traditional samplers*, Thorsons, Wellingborough, 1983

FURBER, ALAN, *Layout and design for calligraphers*, Taplinger Publishing, New York, 1984

GEDDES, ELIZABETH, *Blackwork embroidery*, Mills & Boon, London, 1965

GIERL, IRMGARD, *The Sampler book*, A. & C. Black, London, 1987

GOSTELOW, MARY, *Blackwork*, Van Nostrand Reinhold, New York, 1976

GOURDIE, TOM, *Calligraphic styles*, Taplinger Publishing, New York, 1979

GRAFTON, CAROL BELANGER, *Bizarre and ornamental alphabets*, Dover Publications, New York, 1981

GRAFTON, ELIZABETH BELANGER, *Historic alphabets and initials*, Dover Publications, New York, 1982

JONES, MARY EIRWEN, *British samplers*, B. T. Batsford, London, 1988

KNIGHT, STAN, *Historical scripts: a handbook for calligraphers*, A. & C. Black, London, 1984

LEFÉBURE, ERNEST, *Broderies et dentelles*, Ernest Gründ, Paris, 1926

LUPFER, E. A., *Ornate pictorial calligraphy*, Dover Publications, New York, 1982

Modes et Travaux, *A Sampler of alphabets*, Sterling Publishing, New York, 1987

MUZIKA, FRANTISEK, *Krásné pısmo*, SNKL, Prague, 1963

PARKER, ROZSIKA, *The subversive stitch*, The Women's Press, London, 1984

PASCOE, MARGARET, *Blackwork embroidery*, B. T. Batsford, London, 1986

POTTER, TONY, *Lettering and typography*, Usborne, London, 1987

STRIBLEY, MIRIAM, *The calligraphy source book*, Quarto Publishing, London, 1986

SVENNAS, ELSIE, *A handbook of lettering for stitchers*, Van Nostrand Reinhold, New York, 1973

SWIFT, GAY, *The Batsford's encyclopedia of embroidery*, B. T. Batsford, London, 1988

WILSON, ERICA, *Erica Wilson's embroidery book*, Charles Scribner's Sons, New York, 1973

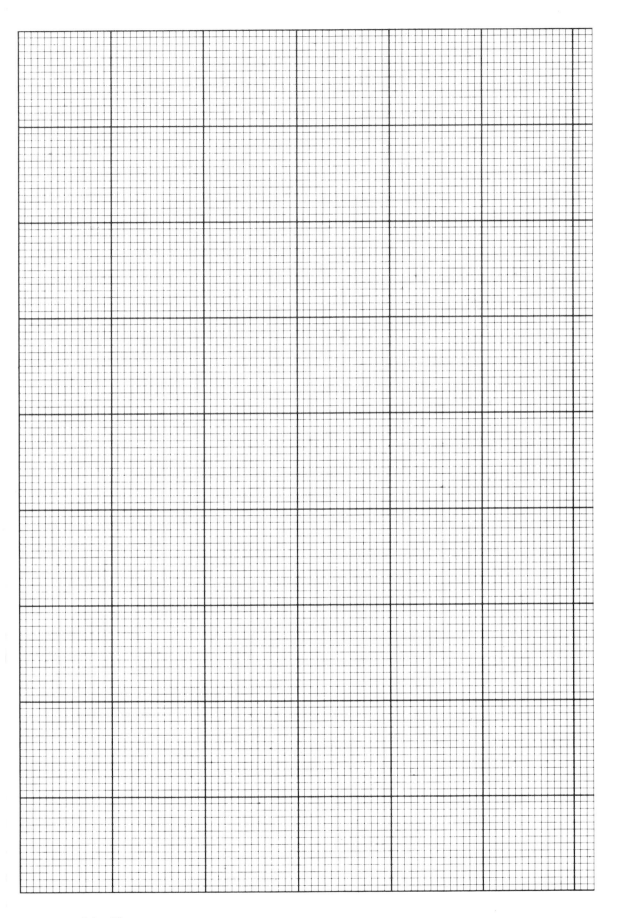

14 : 1″

18 : 1″